SUPPLY SAVVY

scrapbooking

creative ideas for maximizing your scrapbooking stash

by erin lincoln

editor-in-chief • tracy white
founding editor • lisa bearnson
special projects editor • leslie miller
senior editor, special projects • vanessa hoy
senior writer • rachel thomae
associate writer • lori fairbanks
assistant writer • heather jones
copy editor • kim sandoval
editorial assistants • joannie mcbride, fred brewer
art director • brian tippetts
associate art director • erin bayless
photographers • skylar nielsen, gaige redd
co-founder • don lambson

PRIMEDIA
Consumer Magazine & Internet Group

primedia, inc.

chairman • dean nelson
president and ceo • kelly conlin
vice-chairman • beverly c. chell
vp, group publisher • david o'neil
circulation marketing directors • dena spar, janice martin
promotions director • dana smith

primedia outdoor recreation & enthusiast group

president • scott wagner
vp, marketing / internet operations • dave evans

consumer marketing, primedia enthusiast media

vp, single copy marketing • rich baron
vp & cfo, consumer marketing • jennifer prather
vp, retail analysis / development • doug jensen
vp, wholesale / retail • stefan kaiser
vp, consumer marketing operations • elizabeth moss

consumer marketing, enthusiast media subscription company

vp, consumer marketing • bobbi gutman

ISBN 1 929180 93 4

© 2006, PRIMEDIA, Inc

on the cover: sisters
Photo by Hyun-Ae Turner Photography
Supplies *Patterned paper and die cuts:* KI Memories; *Rub-ons:* KI Memories, Making Memories and Doodlebug Design; *Pen:* Pigment Pro by American Crafts; *Brads and metal letter:* Making Memories; *Ribbon:* C.M. Offray & Son; *Other:* Prong fastener.

make
do or do
without

My parents both grew up during the Depression. As a child, I remember how they taught my sisters and me the importance of being frugal. One of their favorite expressions was "Use it up, wear it out, make it do or do without."

While times are better today, my parents' advice still rings true. I always save leftover food for the next day's meal, hand down my kids' clothes to cousins, and save every last piece of unused paper when I scrapbook. However, I will admit that I also love collecting new stuff—especially scrapbook supplies. Of course, a girl needs the latest and greatest paper collection, every new gadget and every font CD to create fabulous pages, right? Well, maybe! If you're like me and want to use all that stuff you've been collecting over the years, you've picked up the right book! I love how Erin Lincoln has filled this book with clever ideas on how you can "use it up, wear it out, make it do or do without," as well as her suggestions on how to combine your favorite classic supplies with those new products you love today. After reading this book, I found myself inspired to try using my classic supplies in a whole new way!

Now, where did I put those adorable stickers from 2002?

Lisa

the challenge: use your stash

Truth be told: I spend just as much time shopping for scrapbooking supplies as I do actually scrapbooking. I love browsing for new products and surfing the Web for the latest releases. And I can totally justify it all to my husband, Matt. Believe me, I've come up with every imaginable excuse in the book as to why scrapbook shopping and the subsequent hoarding of supplies is good for me, my family and society in general. My creativity is not limited to scrapbook pages, I assure you. Unfortunately for me, Matt sees right through it.

After six years of this delinquent behavior, I don't need to tell you just how many scrapbook supplies I've managed to squirrel away in my townhouse. I'm sure you have a pretty good idea. For the most part, I can live in denial about it all and go about my merry way right to the local scrapbook store, wallet in hand. But every now and then, I look around and I just get this sinking feeling in my stomach. So. Much. Stuff. And I bought most of it.

I decided to challenge myself. One hundred layouts done and complete

with the stuff I have in my house. No shopping. No using new supplies. No

sneaking things in when the hubby's at work. And although my dear friend

Lee Anne offered to sneak me the new KI Memories paper, I never took her

up on it. Nope … it was time to face reality and shovel myself out of this

mountain of product.

This book is a result of my challenge to myself to use the product I had on

hand to create layouts I love. My wish of all wishes is that this book will also

inspire you to dig out those old stickers and find a new use for them. Or

that you'll decide that piece of Mustard

Moon paper from 2002 is still cool.

Aged to perfection, you might say.

What once was old is new again.

Reinvent your idea of what's

trendy and what's useful.

You might be surprised with

the results.

Take care and scrap on!

Lincoln

contents

1.
patterned paper

BASICGREY, BO-BUNNY PRESS, IMAGINATION PROJECT, MY MIND'S EYE, NRN DESIGNS, WORLDWIN

She'll decide to go out with friends instead of me on the opening night of the latest chick flick that we've both agreed to see together. She's been only coming home for a few hours every other week...dinner if we're lucky...before she heads back down to school. She's only home until after New Year's before going back to Baltimore to work and stay in the dorms, despite the fact that Christmas break is five weeks long. And yesterday? Well, yesterday she was talking about moving to San Diego and living with Skeeter while she goes to nursing school. I hate to say it, but I just tear up whenever I think of her doing that. I'm literally wiping the tears off my cheeks as I write. Mom says that she's just spreading her wings and becoming an adult. Then she reminds me that I too, did the same. And that now, I know what it was like when I put her through it for the first time. Matt tells me that "Lizzie has to do what is best for Lizzie" as he gives me a hug. And me? What do I say? I say that she's my little sister. That she is one of my favorite people, one of the few that I find completely necessary in my life. That when I'm feeling particularly unselfish, I'll say her happiness trumps my need to have her around. But most of all...I'll say right here and now that I never knew it would hurt so much to see her grow up. I just love her so much. My little sister.

JOURNEY

Miss Independent

She's Trying To Spread Her Wings

miss independent

Supplies *Patterned paper:* SEI; *Copper letters:* Collage Keepsakes, The Card Connection; *Computer fonts:* CK Dandy, "Creative Clips & Fonts for Special Occasions" CD, *Creating Keepsakes*; 2Peas Red Dog, downloaded from *www.twopeasinabucket.com*; Nashville Light, downloaded from the Internet; *Other:* Buttons, label tape and "E" accent.

chapter one

Isn't it in "The Scrapbooker's Creed" somewhere that we can never be satisfied to use something "as is"? We've always got to do something to it, right? Sand it, staple it, rip it, paint it, microwave it. Okay, I was joking on that last one (or at least I won't admit otherwise), but you get the drift. I find myself on a constant quest to alter my scrapbook supplies—but hey, it's a good thing, actually.

I've saved many a piece of vexing patterned paper by grabbing a pair of scissors and cutting particular elements from it. Like I did on this page. See how I transformed a busy pattern into a clever page border? This is an absolutely foolproof technique I use a lot because it's very easy, can "make the page" and takes the place of other more expensive embellishments.

In this chapter, I'll share how I modify, transform, personalize and customize patterned paper and cardstock to make the most of my scrapbooking stash.

available one time only

Supplies *Patterned paper:* Mara-Mi; *Photo turns:* 7gypsies; *Index tab:* Sweetwater; *Snaps:* Making Memories; *Stamping ink:* ColorBox, Clearsnap; *Computer fonts:* 2Peas Tubby and 2Peas Tasklist, downloaded from *www.twopeasinabucket.com.*

quick idea: I used two pieces of the same patterned paper, only in different colors. I cut elements from one and added them to the other to create a visual triangle on my layout. (See the positioning of the green squares?)

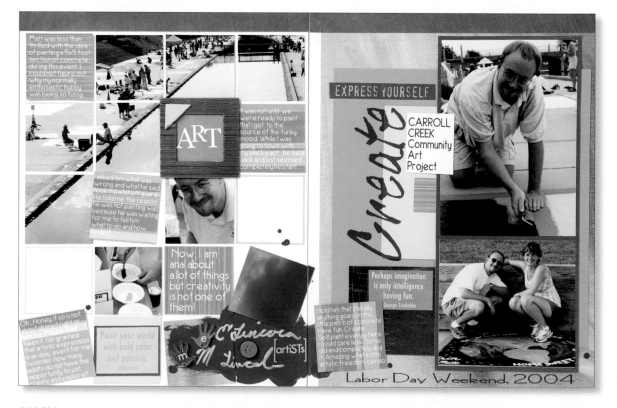

create

Supplies *Patterned papers:* Karen Foster Design, Making Memories and KI Memories; *Rub-ons, acrylic paint, frame, eyelet letter and metal photo corner:* Making Memories; *Pen:* Galaxy Writer, American Crafts; *Computer fonts:* 2Peas Tubby and 2Peas Squish, downloaded from *www.twopeasinabucket.com;* TigerTails, downloaded from the Internet; *Other:* Acrylic hands.

quick idea: I created my journaling blocks by scanning patterned paper, adding white text in Adobe Photoshop and printing it out.

51st birthday

Supplies *Patterned papers:* Daisy D's Paper Co. and Scenic Route Paper Co.; *Rubber stamp:* Hero Arts; *Stamping ink:* VersaMark, Tsukineko; *Charms and acrylic paint:* Making Memories; *Stickers:* Déjà Views by The C-Thru Ruler Co.; *Other:* Metal-rimmed tag and brad.

quick idea: Customize text patterned paper by adding your own words or numbers to it. Notice how I printed my title over the patterned paper.

summer rental

Supplies *Patterned papers:* BasicGrey, Hot Off The Press, Daisy D's Paper Co. and Mustard Moon; *Rub-ons:* Autumn Leaves and KI Memories; *Canvas letters:* Li'l Davis Designs; *Stick pin:* EK Success; *Woven label and date stamp:* Making Memories; *Stamping ink:* StazOn, Tsukineko; *Computer font:* Times New Roman, Microsoft Word; *Other:* Fibers.

quick idea: To fill in the spaces in my photo collage, I cut images of seashells from patterned paper that look like actual photographs.

how to put a dent in your stash of old patterned paper

I've recently come to the conclusion that all the little tips we know about fashion can be applied to scrapbooking—for example, the "something old, something new" principle. That classic white shirt you've had since 1992 can pair well with one of those hip new tweed blazers. And goodness knows, just about anything goes with the J.Crew khakis I've had since college.

The same goes with your scrapbook supplies. In that stack of patterned paper currently being neglected in your stash, I guarantee there are some "classics" just waiting to be paired up with the trendiest papers around. The key? Keep it simple. Pair similar colors. Find several papers that work together and then add a new twist.

For example, on my "Joy" page, I combined a red-dotted paper (after I saw Becky Higgins use it back in the days of Paperkins, I just had to buy 10 sheets of it) and a simple stitched paper. I accented the page with some funky ornament accents. It looks great, and I put a dent in my pile of old 8½" x 11" papers. And that makes me a happy camper.

When you're shopping for new supplies, keep the "something old, something new" principle in mind. Invest more heavily in those products you know you can mix and match with items you already own; however, by no means deprive yourself of the latest piece of trendy patterned paper, because I wouldn't dare ask that of myself or you. Let's face it, 60 cents is a cheap way to gain a bit of happiness. Instead, buy in moderation. If you don't see yourself using it up in the next few months, before something even newer and cooler hits the market, resist the urge to buy 10 sheets. Get one sheet instead.

Every year...
the same
photos
the same
people
the same
presents
the same
laughter
the same
traditions

2004

merry

JOY Christmas Eve

Year in and year out, our Christmas Eve remains constant.

It is only us who change. One year older and even more grateful for our blessings.

joy

Supplies *Patterned papers:* KI Memories and Lasting Impressions for Paper; *Rub-ons:* KI Memories and Déjà Views by The C-Thru Ruler Co.; *Negatives:* Narratives, Creative Imaginations; *Stamping ink:* ColorBox, Clearsnap; *Metal frame:* Nunn Design; *Computer fonts:* CK Letter Home, "Creative Clips & Fonts by Becky Higgins" CD, *Creating Keepsakes*; Times New Roman, Microsoft Word; Belwe BD, Corel WordPerfect.

frederick art festival

Supplies *Patterned papers:* Rhonna Farrer for Autumn Leaves, 7gypsies, Creative Imaginations and Mustard Moon; *Chipboard shapes:* Bazzill Basics Paper; *Transparency:* Design Originals; *Epoxy and wood letters:* Li'l Davis Designs; *Mailbox letters and rub-ons:* Making Memories; *Pen:* Zig Writer, EK Success; *Computer font:* Times New Roman, Microsoft Word; *Other:* Bookplate and brads.

patterned-paper layers

My father is a civil engineer. During childhood vacations, he'd give us geology lessons every time we'd drive through a part of the country where the mountains had been blasted away to create a road or a tunnel. He'd point out the different layers of rock and tell us how each layer represented a different era in time.

Dad would be proud to know that I've taken that lesson and found a way to apply it to my scrap stash. I've been collecting patterned paper for years now and have discovered that each layer of patterned paper represents a different era. For example, the era of black, white, and brown patterned text paper reminds me of the collage craze of 2003. I've mixed that paper with the graphic look (think SEI) popular in the summer of 2002 and the coordinated look (think Chatterbox) so popular in 2004. You may be surprised at just how much fun it can be to create patterned-paper looks from the layers in your stash.

Go ahead and excavate that patterned text paper and put it to some new uses. Add some color by printing or stamping right on top of it. The white and kraft backgrounds disappear and the text remains, resulting in your own personalized designs. It's so easy and a great way to put a new spin on something you already own.

We've been wanting to take Elizabeth to the races ever since she turned 18. Finally, when she was 19 years, 1 month, and 2days old, we managed to cross the state line and place our wagers on our favorite ponies. For a person who majored in animal science, I have no talent in picking out the best horseflesh from the field of 10. Trifeca, exacta, boxing...all Greek to me. I lost all my races, which I think defies some type of statistical law. I figure all my $2 bets were just payment for the entertainment. Elizabeth, however, must have smuggled a lucky horseshoe in, because she picked the right horses to win in a couple races. To soothe my bruised ego, I like to think of it as beginner's luck.

THE EXCITEMENT BEGINS WITH THE BELL!

WIN, PLACE

WE ALL WAIT WITH BATED BREATH FOR THE RESULTS AND THE PAYOFFS TO BE POSTED.

win, place or show

Supplies *Patterned papers:* Chatterbox and Making Memories; *Chipboard comma and buttons:* Making Memories; *Computer fonts:* Times New Roman, Microsoft Word; Falreserif 821 BT, Corel WordPerfect; 2Peas Tasklist, downloaded from www.twopeasinabucket.com; *Other:* Bookplates and brads.

quick idea: The background is a piece of striped patterned paper. I printed my title directly onto the bright-orange strip. This is a good example of building a layout around a piece of patterned paper.

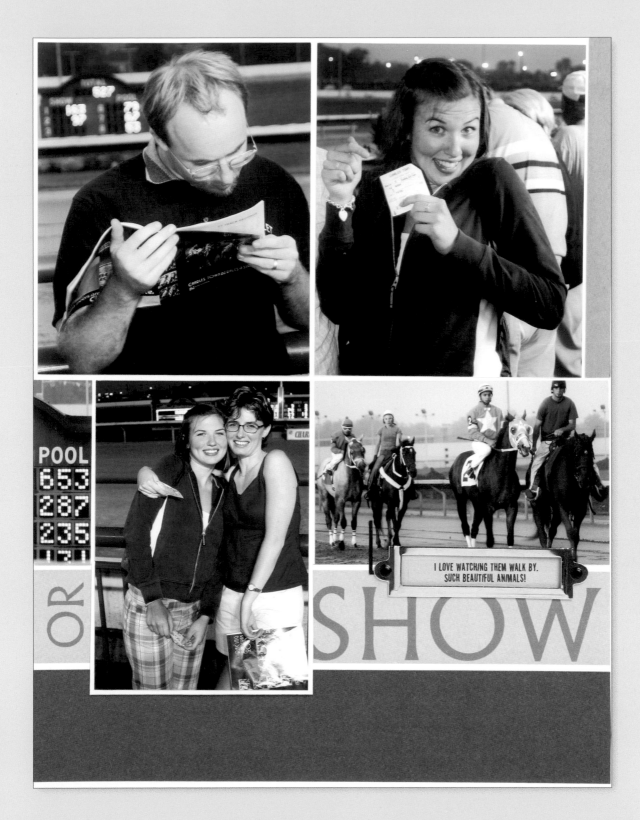

POOL
653
287
235

OR SHOW

I LOVE WATCHING THEM WALK BY.
SUCH BEAUTIFUL ANIMALS!

creativity from your own supply stash

Have you ever hit that creative brick wall when you're working on a layout? You know what I mean. You're working along and then suddenly … nothing. You just can't figure out where to go next. It's frustrating, but the good news is that I've discovered a solution that's 100-percent free. And the best thing about it? You don't even have to leave your scrapbook room.

Here's what works for me. First, I start by just rifling through my stash. I pull out old stuff I've always wanted to use. I make a pile of random patterned papers that just appeal to me. I find a basket and toss embellishments inside until the basket is full. Then I pull out some stickers that have nothing to do with the theme I'm scrapbooking. (Stay with me here, I know it sounds a bit disorganized, but trust me, there's a method to my creative madness.) I kind of make a mess with my supplies. (It's alright, I promise.)

This random and seemingly nonsensical pile of things is what I like to refer to as my "creativity stash." This is a group of items that are fresh in my mind and right in front of me. And because it's all so gloriously random—colors and patterns and shapes are all swirling together—I make combinations I would have never thought of if things were put away nicely. Creative soup right there at my feet. Gotta love it. I'd bet money the one thing you need to finish that layout and make it a real humdinger is right there in that stash.

Keep your creativity stash out for a few days. Make a neat pile of it, but keep it separate from everything else. When it's time to start a new layout, go there first. Some amazing layouts happen this way. After you've tapped this resource for a handful of projects, put it all away. Neat and organized once again, only this time, you got some layouts done in the process without spending a dime.

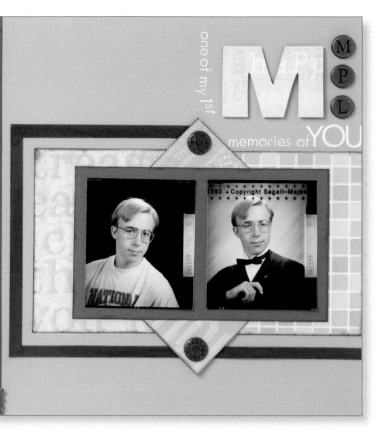

A memory we speak of often is from an afternoon band rehearsal. Matt was a drummer. I played the clarinet. Mr. Rupert cut us all off in the middle of a measure to tell us something. Matt had a tiny little triangle part. He was in charge of a simple "ding, ding, ding"...little sounds which don't usually stand out behind a 65 member band. One might think to be discouraged by having such an insignificant part. Not Matt. He dinged on that triangle like his life depended on it. All the enthusiasm he could muster, he did, and the notes rang out clear and true. Mr. Rupert stopped us all to applaud his effort and use him as an example. His usual teamwork spiel. We'd had heard it all before, a gazillion times. What a dork, I thought. I remember it like it was yesterday.

For all the things I can remember, I find it so odd that this memory is so crystal clear. Why? Because it is just so typical Matt. At the time, I didn't realize it...but now, having been with him for ten years, I can see it as a moment that can be used to define him. He is so enthusiastic about everything....work, play, love, laughter, banging on that stupid little triangle. He holds nothing back...ever. OK, so maybe sometimes I still think he's a bit dorky, but now I can appreciate the motives behind certain actions. I'm so lucky that I have this memory of him, one that predates "us" by a whole year. It speaks of his true nature, one uninfluenced by me, and one of the reasons why I fell in love with him. I'm in love with him still for many different reasons, most of them tangled up in this thing called "us"...but this...this was all him and I remember it so well.

just my **thoughts**

one of my 1st

M **M** **P** **L**

memories of **YOU**

first memory of you

Supplies *Patterned paper, copper letter and sticker:* K&Company; *Rub-ons:* Making Memories and Autumn Leaves; *Brads and chipboard letter:* Making Memories; *Stamping ink:* ColorBox, Clearsnap; *Computer font:* 2Peas Tubby, downloaded from www.twopeasinabucket.com.

my one and only goal

Supplies *Patterned papers:* Mustard Moon and Marcella by Kay for Target; *Transparency:* Daisy D's Paper Co.; *Stickers:* Inspire ME and Sticker Studio; *Rub-ons:* Autumn Leaves and Making Memories; *Computer fonts:* CK Urban, "Fresh Fonts" CD, *Creating Keepsakes*; 2Peas Tasklist, downloaded from www.twopeasinabucket.com; Fenice BT, downloaded from the Internet; *Other:* Paper clasp.

quick idea Use lined patterned paper as a template for lining up your journaling.

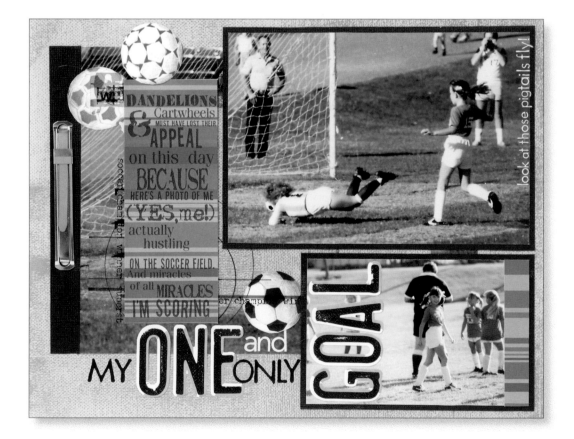

DANDELIONS & Cartwheels MUST HAVE LOST THEIR APPEAL on this day BECAUSE HERE'S A PHOTO OF ME (YES, me!) actually hustling ON THE SOCCER FIELD And miracles of all MIRACLES I'M SCORING

look at those pigtails fly!

MY **ONE** and **ONLY** **GOAL**

skeeter

Supplies *Patterned papers:* The Robin's Nest and The Paper Patch; *Rub-ons:* Scrapperware, Creative Imaginations; *Snap and eyelet word:* Making Memories; *Transfer pen:* Eberhard Faber; *Computer font:* CK Evolution, "Fresh Fonts" CD, *Creating Keepsakes; Other:* Washers, slides and eyelets.

step-by-step:
patterned-paper transfer

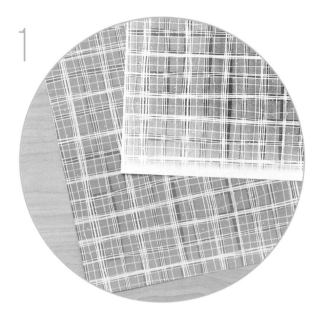

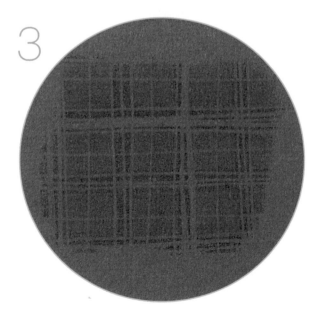

Turn some of that old paper into a texture-transfer medium for your cardstock. Make a black-and-white photocopy of the paper and then transfer the pattern with a blending pen onto cardstock. Here's how:

1. Make a black-and-white photocopy of your patterned paper. A print of a scan will not work, as the printer toner will not transfer.

2. Lay the photocopy face down on your cardstock. Repeatedly "write" on the back of the photocopy with a photo-transfer pen. The piece of paper will become very wet.

3. Lift off the photocopy to see your design transferred to your cardstock.

note: *Do this in a well-ventilated area—the fumes from the photo-transfer pen are very strong.*

National

World War II

ATLANTIC

Memorial

Washington, D.C.

Don, Red, Jim, Clyde, Mike (Chuck, not pictured)
Mayer Brothers

At the memorial, there is a wall full of gold stars on a field of blue. Too many to count. Each star represents 1000 American lives lost in the war. The number is staggering. And then to think that my grandfather and his 5 brothers all served during that time and that all 6 came home alive and whole. It's against all odds that these brothers grew into old men. So at the memorial we not only paid our respects, but reflected on our blessings. It would have been a different world if fate had dealt another hand to the Mayer brothers.

They All Came Home

mayer brothers

Supplies *Patterned paper:* Making Memories; *Vellum:* Paper Adventures; *Die cut:* Memories in Uniform; *Slide:* Design Originals; *Epoxy sticker:* K&Company; *Star clip art:* Downloaded from the Internet; *Computer fonts:* Times New Roman, Microsoft Word; Texas Hero, downloaded from the Internet; Belwe BD, Corel WordPerfect.

patterned-paper challenge

You would think I'd have more cardstock-only pages, but I have the tendency to reach for all that lovely patterned paper first when I start a page. Do you find yourself doing the same? Buck the trend and do a cardstock-only page instead. You'll find that doing the opposite of what you usually do is a great way to jumpstart your scrapbooking creativity.

Monochromatic color choices make it easy and add depth to your layout. Use a precut page, like Making Memories' Perspectives, and it becomes a no-brainer … and don't we all need one of those every now and again? For all of you cardstock-only users, we'll now return to our regularly scheduled programming, where we insist you use all that patterned paper up. That's right, I want to see 20 layouts using patterned paper before you can even think of touching that cardstock. Got it?

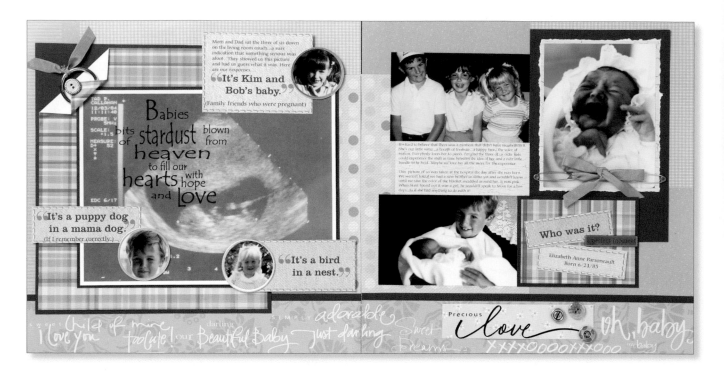

precious love

Supplies *Patterned papers:* K&Company, Daisy D's Paper Co., Pebbles Inc. and Provo Craft; *Sticker:* Bo-Bunny Press; *Metal buttons:* K&Company; *Rub-ons:* Déjà Views by The C-Thru Ruler Co.; *Eyelet word:* Making Memories; *Computer font:* Times New Roman, Microsoft Word; *Other:* Ribbon, eyelets, safety pins and metal-rimmed tags.

quick idea: I'll let you in on a little secret … it took me several tries to come up with just the right combination of patterned papers for this layout. It's always trial and error for me—so don't be afraid to experiment until you find the combination that clicks.

delicious

Supplies *Patterned papers:* BasicGrey, Daisy D's Paper Co., Scenic Route Paper Co., Mustard Moon and Flair Designs; *Black letters:* K&Company; *Buttons:* 7gypsies; *Pen:* Zig Scroll & Brush, EK Success; *Computer fonts:* Engravrs Roman BT and Texas Hero, downloaded from the Internet; *Other:* Ribbon.

quick idea: Cut your paper into shapes inspired by your photographs. The awning on the restaurant patio inspired my scallop border.

pretty

Supplies *Patterned papers:* SEI, O'Scrap!, KI Memories and Karen Foster Design; *Watch crystal and acrylic accent:* KI Memories; *Buttons:* American Crafts; *Stamping ink:* ColorBox, Clearsnap; *Stitching template:* Li'l Davis Designs; *Rubber stamp and acrylic paint:* Making Memories; *Computer fonts:* 2Peas Tubby, 2Peas Sweetpea and 2Peas Fairy Princess, downloaded from *www.twopeasinabucket.com*.

quick idea: All the paper strips on this page have the same color in common: hot pink.

from just one piece
of patterned paper

I went to the CK Arizona Scrapbook Convention last fall. I'm not sure if you've ever been to the "Land of the Rising Sun," but if you have, you know they probably should come up with a different state motto. Isn't "Land of 1,001 Fabulous Scrapbook Stores" so much more appropriate? Oh, man … it was nirvana. I'm not one with a whole lot of self-discipline, so you can just imagine how nuts I went.

My buddy Christine was my accomplice. We made one serious shopping tag team. She did pretty well keeping up with this shopping machine, but I remember her giving me a little bit of flack over a particular piece of yellow and purple patterned paper. I got a "whatever are you going to do with that?" type of look. So I only bought one. Now, I know most people like to buy a minimum of two pieces of paper for a two-page spread. After all, you don't want to run out, right? Okay. Stop with those thoughts. Even without realizing it, you've already subconsciously started planning your layout: using the same patterned paper on both sides. In giving yourself extra, you're almost limiting yourself. Now imagine doing that every time you go shopping.

Here's my challenge. Find a single piece of patterned paper in your stash and do two projects with it. The hard part? Try to use as much of that paper as you can on your two pieces, as I did here with my "Hawaii" layout and "Thank You Card." Chances are, I'll never find pictures that will match this paper again. I don't have many reasons for such a fun tropical theme, so the one sheet worked just perfectly for me.

I know I always start pages the same way. Do you? Necessity is the mother of invention, so expect to forge a new path with this exercise. This is a great way to find a different angle on your creativity and get you out of the "need multiple sheets" mentality.

hawaii

Supplies *Patterned papers:* Creative Imaginations, NRN Designs and Paperfever; *Frames and letters:* Forget Me Not Designs; *Epoxy frame and metal setting:* Li'l Davis Designs; *Stickers:* K&Company; *Rub-ons:* Chartpak; *Snaps and washer:* Making Memories; *Computer fonts:* Times New Roman, Microsoft Word; Bell Gothic, downloaded from the Internet; *Other:* Wood beads and handmade paper.

thank you purse card

Supplies *Patterned papers:* NRN Designs and Creative Imaginations; *Letter stamps:* Savvy Stamps; *Stamping ink:* Distress Ink, Ranger Industries; *Leather bookplate, eyelets and snap:* Making Memories; *Punches:* EK Success; *Die-cut frame:* Forget Me Not Designs; *Computer font:* Engravrs Roman BT, downloaded from the Internet.

The Final Stop in My Waitressing Career

GRIFF'S landing

Good Food, Good Friends, Good Tips!

I'd wait tables again in a heartbeat

Of course, there was a few down ... The one and only Griff ... butt once when I ... my drinks at the ...

Griff's was a nice seafood place, as well as a bar. I lea... A LOT about drinks (oys... ...yone) and handling ... ...t either o...

We had to wear a pair of khaki pants or shorts and a Gri... My favorite was my n... sleeveless one. Dur...

Thursday Nights
2 Doubles on the Weekend

griff's landing

Supplies *Patterned papers:* Sonburn, Karen Foster Design and 7gypsies; *Index tab:* 7gypsies; *Stickers:* Chatterbox; *Twill:* Creek Bank Creations; *Ribbon:* Textured Trios, Michaels; *Brads and jump rings:* Making Memories; *Computer fonts:* Times New Roman, Microsoft Word; 2Peas Squish, downloaded from *www.twopeasinabucket.com*; *Other:* Bottle caps, fake credit cards, matchbook, coins and magnet strips.

a little bit of patterned paper

This page is going to do nothing but tell you what a total and complete packrat I am. See that itsy bitsy little strip of patterned paper with a "food" theme down there on the lower-left-hand side? I can't tell you how many times I've run across it in my stash over the years when I was doing a clean and purge. And every time, it survived the cleaning rampage. Several sheets of it, no less. I just keep telling myself that one day, on a very special page, I'll get around to using it.

And the real kicker of it is that it's border paper. Really dates it, doesn't it? But by using just the edge of it and adding a few trendy touches, it works fine. It's very appropriate to the page. Bottom line is this: Don't feel like you have to get rid of a piece of paper just because others think it's the height of uncool. If there's something you like and something you think you will use one day, keep it.

TAGALONG

1 Tag heard a rumor that 25% of cats get to have all the cat nip they want. He asked around the neighborhood and found that of the 24 cats he asked, 9 said they get all the catnip they want. Test Tag's claim (the rumor) at a=0.02 significance level.

WORD PROBLEM

2 Furgus is the proud father of 8 kittens which is a real trick because he is neutered...but hey, let him live the dream. 5 kittens are girls, which all look alike, and 3 kittens are boys which each look very different. Furgus lines up the new kittens for inspection by Tag, his brother. How many unique arrangements are possible as far as Tag is concerned? Remember, Tag will not be able to tell the girl kittens apart.

Murphy is trying to convince the other cats that he eats at most 0.75 lbs. of food/day. Furgus mentions that in the last 20 days, Murphy has averaged 0.83 lbs. of food/day. The standard deviation for daily consumption of cat food is known to be 0.2 lbs. Test Murphy's claim at the a=0.01 significance level. **3**

CAT •MATH

cat math

Supplies *Patterned papers and transparency:* Karen Foster Design; *Stickers:* Pebbles Inc.; *Letter stamps and rub-on:* Making Memories; *Tags and tacks:* Chatterbox; *Ribbon:* Bobbin Ribbon; *Chipboard letters:* Li'l Davis Designs; *Stamping ink:* ColorBox, Clearsnap; *Pen:* Galaxy Marker, American Crafts; *Pop dots:* All Night Media; *Computer fonts:* Comic Sans, Microsoft Word; CK Neat Print, "Creative Clips & Fonts for Special Occasions" CD, *Creating Keepsakes; Other:* Index card tablet.

quick idea: I created the clipboard on my page by cutting a clipboard image from a piece of paper by Karen Foster Design.

When Mr. Lincoln comes home he faces the decision of which cat to try to pet first. 40% of the time he chooses Tag, 35% of the time Furgus, and 25% of the time he pets Murphy. However the cats have a tendency to run away when Mr. Lincoln tries to pick them up. Tag does this 5% of the time, Furgus 10%, and Murphy 35%. What is the possibility that Mr. Lincoln will pet Furgus first today when he gets home?

more problems

Who Was There: Mommy and Daddy and the Vanderhursts

What We Did: You ate cake and ice cream and went to watch the 4th of July fireworks (which you didn't like)

Gifts: Talking Winnie, ABC Blocks, wagon, stuffed turtle, Chatter phone, pull and push toys.

Happy Birthday Sweetheart! It is hard to believe that you are already three years old! I sure hope that you had fun at your birthday party and that you enjoyed all of your little friends (Peter and Christine Townley, Peter Jereb, Mike and John West, Skeeter, Jeannine, and Grammie and Papa).

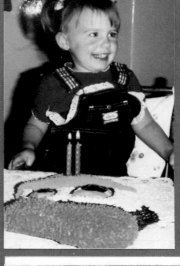

Grandma and Grandpa were here to help you celebrate your 2nd birthday. What a big girl you are. Mama made you a Donald Duck birthday cake. You received many presents too...tricycle, puzzles, Weeble House, clothes, and books. What a special day it was for you!

1 2 3 4 5 6

Supplies *Patterned papers, tacks, die-cut frames and title plate*: Chatterbox; *Computer font*: 2Peas Tubby, downloaded from *www.twopeasinabucket.com; Other*: Ribbon and envelope.

quick idea: Cut patterned paper into strips and use them to divide your layout into sections.

birthday

4 5 6

Happy Birthday Erin! Sure do hope you had a fun party. Friends at your party were: Lewis & Issac de la Fuente, Peter and Christine Townley, Danielle & Nicole Laurent, Peter Jereb, and Skeeter & Jeannine. We had lunch (hots dogs, chips, punch) and everyone tried to break the clown pinata. Presents were opened and cake and ice cream cones were served to all your little friends.

What a happy birthday girl you are. It's hard to believe that you are five years old. Grandma and Grandpa Mayer were here to celebrate. Your friend Stacy Davies came over for dinner and a rainbow birthday cake. Gifts were clothes and an Orange Juice doll.

We just moved into our new house in Santa Maria. What an exciting weekend & holiday! There are so many new friends in the neighborhood to help celebrate your birthday this year. You had cake & ice cream out in front of the house during the neighborhood block party. What a treat that was. Happy Birthday to a very special little girl. We love you Erin!

2.
stickers
and die cuts

"us"

Erin · Michele · Parsoneault · Peter · Lincoln · Matthew

empl

This is 'so' high school and we both know it. But it is also 'so' Matt and Erin. Thus we love it. I was probably doodling in calculus class once upon a time when I discovered how our initials overlap. We each have two letters in common, making two names one. And ever since, it's how we refer to this thing called 'us.' Completely dorky EMPL 4EVER

empl
Supplies *Patterned paper:* Deluxe Designs; *Stickers:* American Crafts and me & my BIG ideas; *Letters:* Doodlebug Design; *Pen:* Zig Scroll & Brush, EK Success; *Computer fonts:* 2Peas Hot Chocolate, downloaded from *www.twopeasinabucket.com*; CK Retro Block, "Heritage, Vintage & Retro Collection" CD and CK Neat Print, "Creative Clips & Fonts for Special Occasions" CD, *Creating Keepsakes*; *Other:* Metal-rimmed tags.

chapter two

I get inspiration everywhere: magazines, print ads, television shows, songs. But why not get inspired by something closer to home—your very own scrapbook stash? It's a simple and easy-to-access source of tremendous creative stimulation. Theme stickers, metal words and die cuts can all spark the flames of ingenuity.

For example, the angle on this layout came while I was sitting at my computer, trying to figure out which letters I wanted to order from a new paper line. Don't ask me why I never thought of doing this page before then—the whole "EMPL" thing is totally scrapworthy. It made me wonder what other products were hiding in my closet that would give me a similar "why didn't I think of that before?" moment. I wanted to be open to the possibilities.

And did you notice? I used some ancient stickers by me & my BIG ideas (MAMBI) on this layout. I never got rid of them because I figured dots could never go out of style. I drew a circle using a bowl as a template and placed the stickers evenly around it.

What else can you do with the older accents in your scrap stash? In this chapter, I'll show you numerous ideas that will help you purge your stash, sending the embellishments to your album and not the donation pile.

perfectly
coordinated die cuts

Laser die cuts can be a little tricky to use sometimes, because they come in very specific colors. I was lucky when I scored this die cut of the exact helicopter my brother trained in. I just had to use it—mostly because I knew he'd get a kick out of it when he saw the layout for the first time. The only problem? While accurate to real life, the orange from the original die cut was a little bright for my photos. I chose a better suited shade from my cardstock stash, traced the orange section from the die cut and cut it out (after blowing the dust off of my X-acto knife). I even created a matching border from the leftover cardstock.

Now, I wouldn't recommend using this technique for all die cuts ever manufactured, as they can be fairly intricate, but this might help you out in a pinch. If you can use one die cut this way, feel triumphant. It just means one less item in your stash.

helo pilot

Supplies *Patterned papers:* American Crafts and Chatterbox; *Letters and tiles:* Junkitz; *Rub-ons:* Autumn Leaves and Making Memories; *Die cut:* Memories in Uniform; *Computer font:* 2Peas Tubby, downloaded from *www.twopeasinabucket.com*; *Other:* Plastic canvas and metal washers.

3 KIDS

Puzzles SESAME STREET Swing Sets RAGGEDY ANN DOLLS Grandparent Visits GO FAST TENNIES Park Visits STROLLER FOR THREE Nursery Rhymes HIDE N' SEEK Osh Kosh B'Gosh KIDDIE POOLS Crayons RECORD PLAYER Kitchen Set WOODEN BLOCKS Catching Bugs SHARING ROOMS All 3 in the Tub MACARONI & CHEESE Knee Socks WIGGLE WORM Fishing MRS. SISCO Annie FOX AND THE HOUND Richard Scary Books WEEBLE WOBBLES Homemade Dresses PUSH UP POPS Sewing Cards HAIR RIBBONS Visiting Dad's Office AFTERNOON NAPS Beanie Weenie Casserole THE BLANKET Show Muppets TREE SWING Trips to Medford MITTENS ON A STRING Feeding Ducks HOT CYCLES Disco Mickey Mouse SHOOTS & LADDERS Sandbox MEMORY GAME Finding Gold Bug STRIDE RITES Training Wheels COLORING BOOKS

Growing Up Parsoneault

Skeeter Jeannine Erin

growing up parsoneault

Supplies *Patterned papers:* The Paper Loft, Kangaroo and Joey, Pebbles Inc., me & my BIG ideas and Scenic Route Paper Co.; *Die cuts:* Close To My Heart and EK Success; *Eyelets and acrylic sticker:* Creative Imaginations; *Button:* Junkitz; *Stickers:* Chatterbox; *Wooden flower:* Li'l Davis Designs; *Metal rings:* 7gypsies; *Punches:* EK Success; *Computer fonts:* 2 Peas Tubby and 2Peas Tasklist, downloaded from *www.twopeasinabucket.com; Other:* Ribbon, staples and embroidery floss.

quick idea: If the colors of your die cuts are too bright for your layout, mute them with a sheet of vellum.

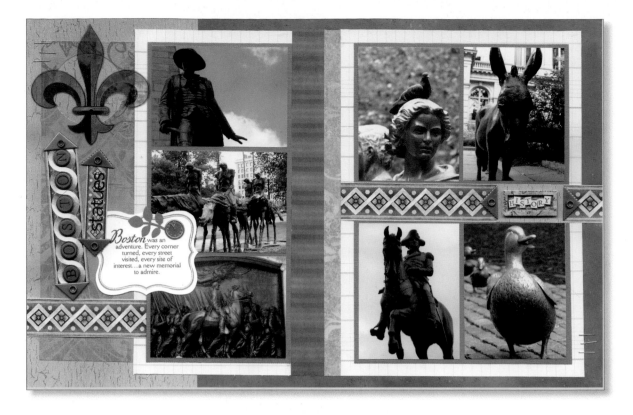

boston statues

Supplies *Patterned papers:*
Carolee's Creations, K&Company,
Déjà Views by The C-Thru Ruler Co.,
Making Memories, Design Originals
and Provo Craft; *Stickers:* Magenta,
Making Memories and K&Company;
Rub-ons and metal photo corners:
Making Memories; *Metal letters:*
K&Company; *Transparency:* Magic
Scraps; *Metal tacks:* EK Success;
Punch: Punch Bunch; *Other:* Charm
and staples.

quick idea: When going
through your stash, pay attention
to product shapes and dimensions.
You'll be surprised at how many
things match each other. On my
layout, the metal photo corners fit
my sticker border perfectly—it looks
like they were made to go together.

lost in translation

Supplies *Patterned papers:*
BasicGrey and KI Memories; *Letter
stickers:* BasicGrey; *Letter stamp:*
Impress Rubber Stamps; *Stamping
ink:* Nick Bantock, Ranger
Industries; *Embossing powder:*
Stampin' Up!; *Pen:* Pigment Pro,
American Crafts; *Computer font:*
Avant Garde, Corel WordPerfect;
Other: Plastic-coated wire and
flower stamps.

start with stickers

I have old supplies that I just love too much to throw out, and
I'm always on the lookout for ways to put them to work. These
border stickers are a perfect example. An easy way to use them is as the
foundation for a layout. Pick paper, photos and accents to match. Yes, it
might be a little untraditional to start a page this way. But as long as you keep
the page authentic (these really are my New Year's resolutions), it simply becomes a
different launching pad for your layout. Remember, a done page is just that—done.
It doesn't matter how you got there.

my resolutions

Supplies *Patterned papers:* Anna Griffin and Colors By Design; *Stickers:* Pebbles Inc. and Creative Imaginations;
Eyelet word, foam stamps and acrylic paint: Making Memories; *Stamping ink:* ColorBox, Clearsnap; VersaMark,
Tsukineko; *Embossing powder:* Stampin' Up!; *Punch:* EK Success; *Hook and eyelets:* Prym-Dritz; *Computer fonts:*
2Peas Squish, downloaded from *www.twopeasinabucket.com*; Times New Roman, Microsoft Word.

That time of year again! New Year's Resolutions. I'm not
sure if that's a good thing or a bad thing ...HA! Last year was
a bit of an success for me as far as goals went, so I decided
"what the heck...let's up the ante a little bit" by adding a few
more. Make life interesting by picking things to work on
that are a bit tough for me. Like patience. I so want patience
RIGHT NOW! And sugar, my beloved sugar. Sigh. I'm not
cutting it out completely, just trying not to go rummaging
around for it on an hourly basis. I want to run my 2nd 5K this
summer. It's good incentive to stay in shape. The more
people I tell about it, the less likely I am to wimp out. And
traditions...we have a few little things that make living at
special, but I'd like to do some more. They
define us as a family. So there you go, my goals for the year.
The scrapbook page is done and there's no going back now.
Photos 1/1/05, Journaling 1/9/05

adding dimension to flat embellishments

Fresh Cuts … yet another product I bought too much of because: (1) they were cheap, and (2) I was completely in love with them. Rebecca Sower just rocks, doesn't she? I bet she could design a good-looking dyed-noodle photo frame, circa my kindergarten years, and I'd buy a dozen of them.

I took Rebecca's lead from the design of the accents and added some dimensional elements to mine. The ribbon and jump rings bring enough of a personal edge to make me feel creative, but I didn't have to invest too much time and work into the embellishments as a whole. I like the arrangement as well.

And remember, just because something has a collage look doesn't mean you can't work it into a more graphic style. Lined up and grounded, these accents become a great part of the page as a whole.

when the price is right

Supplies *Patterned papers:* Sweetwater, Paper Adventures, Mustard Moon and Making Memories; *Jump rings, ribbon and leather frame:* Making Memories; *Stickers and die cuts:* EK Success; *Buttons:* Junkitz; *Computer font:* 2Peas Tasklist, downloaded from *www.twopeasinabucket.com.*

everything and anything rainbow

Supplies *Patterned papers:* KI Memories and American Crafts; *Frame:* Scrapworks; *Punch:* EK Success; *Stickers:* Stamping Station, Tumblebeasts and Chatterbox; *Rub-ons:* K&Company; *Acrylic circle:* Junkitz; *Computer font:* 2Peas Tubby, downloaded from *www.twopeasinabucket.com.*

quick idea: Fold over border stickers and hide the ends under cardstock for a dimensional look.

furgus

Supplies *Patterned papers:* Karen Foster Design and Making Memories; *Stickers:* Karen Foster Design; *Letter stamps:* Ma Vinci's Reliquary; *Stamping ink:* ColorBox, Clearsnap; Stampin' Up!; *Snap and metal corner:* Making Memories; *Pog and folder:* Autumn Leaves; *Other:* Mini folders.

quick idea: Put letter stickers in your journaling for a fun look. Just test-print your journaling so you can make sure the stickers will fit. Trust me on this one … I speak from experience.

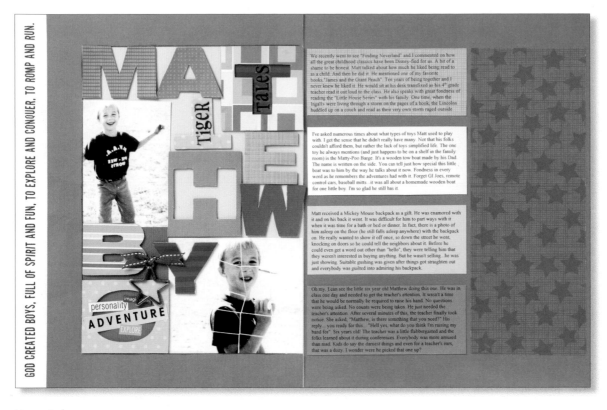

tiger tales

Supplies *Patterned papers:* Chatterbox; *Chipboard letters and letter stickers:* Making Memories; *Stickers:* me & my BIG ideas; *Charm:* Karen Foster Design; *Ribbon:* Bobbin Ribbon and Michaels; *Computer fonts:* 2Peas Tasklist, downloaded from *www.twopeasinabucket.com*; Times New Roman, Microsoft Word.

quick idea: Use up your old chipboard letters by turning a title into a word collage. Because you've used them up, you won't have any guilt when you want to buy the latest chipboard letters.

key points
to remember

Supplies *Stickers:* Pebbles Inc.; *Metal letter:* EK Success; *Eyelets:* Making Memories; *Other:* Ribbon, key and key ring.

quick idea: I mounted border stickers on cardstock, bent them in half and sewed the edges to create pockets.

double-duty accents

This page came a long way from the pink and mint-green 12" x 12" disaster I had started out fussing over. It took me a good hour to realize it just wasn't working. That's when I pulled out this green piece of 8½" x 11" cardstock instead. The smaller size just seemed to click better—and green is one of my tried-and-true shades. (You always need to keep some of those around!)

The big "B" on this page is the only remnant from my original layout, and I like how the flower sticker weaves through it. It makes it more than just the first letter in my title, but rather an embellished element that gives my layout the extra polish it needed. The bookplate further cements the letter's dual purpose, forcing you to look deeper into the layout to see the overall design.

grandma bonnie

Supplies *Patterned papers:* Daisy D's Paper Co. and K&Company; *Stickers:* EK Success and K&Company; *Foam stamp, bookplate and brads:* Making Memories; *Rubber stamp:* Limited Edition Rubberstamps; *Stamping ink:* Distress Ink, Ranger Industries; *Computer fonts:* Schneidler Md BT and Avant Garde Bk BT, Corel WordPerfect; *Other:* Button.

I was driving Mom to the airport so she could catch her flight to Pensacola for Skeet's winging. On the way, she told me this little story about a conversation she had with him that same morning. She couldn't stop herself from tearing up a little bit. And I don't blame her in the least. Tears were invented for moments like these.

Skeeter told Mom that he had awoken that morning and looked over to his desk. There, not yet worn, were his wings. He had purchased them the day before. And as he lay there, he couldn't help but think that those were the very things he had wanted ever since he was a little boy...and now they were his. To wear proudly. With honor. He had achieved his dream.

THE UNITED STATES
NAVY

the united states navy

Supplies *Patterned papers:* Autumn Leaves, Scrapping Times and K&Company; *Page pebble:* Making Memories; *Sticker:* Sticker Studio; *Punch:* EK Success; *Computer fonts:* 2Peas Hot Chocolate, downloaded from *www.twopeasinabucket.com*; Bodoni BT, downloaded from the Internet; *Other:* Car window sticker.

quick idea: I always back my stickers with white cardstock. Then I can move them around on my page at will, without any initial commitment.

u of md

Supplies *Patterned papers:* Daisy D's Paper Co., K&Company and SEI; *Stickers:* Colorbök and EK Success; *Die cuts:* Carolee's Creations; *Rubber stamp and stamping ink:* Stampin' Up!; *Woven label:* me & my BIG ideas; *Closure accent:* Colorbök; *Pen:* Pigment Pro, American Crafts; *Pop dots:* All Night Media; *Computer fonts:* Belwe MD BT and Souvenir Lt BT, Corel WordPerfect; *Other:* Ribbon.

quick idea: With some scanning, resizing and reorienting, die cuts that scream "not me!" can turn into the perfect page accent.

feeding the duckies

Supplies *Patterned papers:* SEI, KI Memories and Chatterbox; *Vellum:* American Crafts; *Rub-ons:* K&Company; *Flower:* Making Memories; *Stamping ink:* ColorBox, Clearsnap; *Computer fonts:* 2Peas Sweetpea, downloaded from *www.twopeasinabucket.com*; Times New Roman, Microsoft Word; Georgia, Corel WordPerfect; *Other:* Embroidery floss and letter beads.

take a chance

I have a sickness. What is it? I have a hard time using something as is—it just isn't in my creative playlist. Occasionally it blows up in my face, and I end up ruining an item that I have only one of. But most of the time, it works out wonderfully.

Go ahead and take that chance with your supplies. What's the worst that can happen? You might have to run to the scrapbook store and replace an embellishment, but you've learned something in the process. So get out the scissors, splash on some paint, sand it until your arm falls off … the only requirement is that you have a good time.

Case in point: When gathering supplies for "Feeding the Duckies" (pg. 52), I found a cute green frame set that included two identical accents. On a whim, I cut apart the frame and used it as a border. I used one of the accents as is. Okay, maybe not "as is" since I placed the "niece" beads across it, but as close as I can get. The other accent? Well, I was only interested in using one button from it to complete my flower on the right side of the layout. Don't mind me—that's just my perfectionist nature coming out again. I've come to accept it about myself.

no photos?
no problem!

In my perfect world, I would have had a professional photographer following me every day since my birth, taking shot after candid shot of my life. Every event would be beautifully photographed and have me in it. It would make for one awesome "All About Me" book, no? Reality, however, leaves a bit to be desired, and I often have to finagle ways of getting myself into shots or just opt not to have photos altogether. That doesn't mean these moments aren't scrapworthy, and I try to scrap them anyway.

In fact, these opportunities are great ways to really let my imagination fly while putting a nice dent in my scrap stash as well. In these instances, stickers are a great choice as accents, because one would be hard pressed to not find a sticker that would fit your given theme. You name it, I bet you can find it.

Set the old "make your photos take center stage" adage aside and let those stickers shine. Make them the focus and nobody will even notice that you don't have a photo to accompany that great story that's just begging to be told.

The pink leotard and dainty little dance slippers, of course. Every six year old's dream. And life was made even sweeter if on our way to or fro from lessons, Mom had to run a few errands. That way,

What was my favorite?

I could preen in front of strangers...
dance my way down the cereal aisle,
and twirl in the check out line.
Look at me! I'm a ballerina!!!!
Everybody look at me!

And when I got home....well, my little sister didn't have a pink leotard OR a pair of slippers. Driving her a little insane with jealousy was certainly not in conflict with the agreed upon rules of sibling warfare. Eat your heart out, you three year old.

Beauty

ballet

Everything that didn't directly involve the aforementioned pink leotard and ballet slippers. Even then, I was not one for activities that required any athletic skill whatsoever. Or a fan of anything that required me to take orders from anyone. I don't plie on command. At six, I knew this. Now at twenty seven, I don't think my basic needs in these categories have changed.

What wasn't....

After three weeks of complaining about going to class, I got out of it. *"My feet hurt"* was a favorite complaint. I used *"I have a headache"* a few times and Mom eventually got the point . Of course, these are ailments I acquired AFTER I had dressed for class. That way I could lounge in my room and read, yet STILL be a ballerina...which was much more my speed.

ballet

Supplies *Patterned papers:* Daisy D's Paper Co. and Keeping Memories Alive; *Stickers:* Scrappin' Dreams, K&Company and Making Memories; *Word embellishment:* K&Company; *Decorative scissors:* Provo Craft; *Computer font:* Times New Roman, Microsoft Word; *Other:* Embroidery fabric, brooch pins, ribbon and staples.

no redemption today

Supplies *Patterned papers:* BasicGrey and Daisy D's Paper Co.; *Stickers:* Karen Foster Design and Boxer Scrapbook Productions; *Page pebbles, eyelet numbers and acrylic paint:* Making Memories; *Pen:* Slick Writer, American Crafts; *Computer font:* Times New Roman, Microsoft Word.

quick idea: Add words to your stickers to make them more appropriate for your page theme.

relax

Supplies *Patterned papers:* Patchwork Paper Design, Daisy D's Paper Co., Mustard Moon, Making Memories and Sweetwater; *Rub-ons:* Autumn Leaves and Making Memories; *Stitching template:* Junkitz; *Embossing powder:* Stampin' Up!; *Sticker:* Making Memories; *Bookplate:* Li'l Davis Designs; *Computer fonts:* CK Typewriter and CK Stencil, "Fresh Fonts" CD, *Creating Keepsakes.*

quick idea: Sometimes the perfect quote or saying can be found on a sticker. If the sticker doesn't match your layout, simply draw inspiration from it when you design your page.

dream house

Supplies *Patterned paper:* me & my BIG ideas; *Stickers:* EK Success, Pebbles Inc. and Karen Foster Design; *Foam letter stamps and acrylic paint:* Making Memories; *Vellum quote:* K&Company; *Eyelets:* Creative Imaginations; *Decoupage medium:* Mod Podge, Plaid Enterprises; *Pen:* Slick Writer, American Crafts; *Other:* Images from magazines.

quick idea: Give your photo stickers a little dimension by putting them on an adhesive dot. And remember, adhesive dots are stickers, too.

ground your stickers

Grounding stickers can work wonders in preventing the dreaded sticker-sneeze syndrome. Place them inside shapes with strong lines for an easy look. In doing so, you give them a place to belong and integrate them into the overall page design.

On a humorous note, I had originally mounted the head of a MAMBI kids sticker on the platter in my title (between "Boiled" and "Head"). It was hilarious, but I just couldn't do that to the poor sticker. MAMBI kids served us well. I needed to show my respect for a job well done.

halloween at the lincolns
Supplies *Patterned papers:* Karen Foster Design and Scenic Route Paper Co.; *Stickers:* Karen Foster Design and Pebbles Inc.; *Button:* Making Memories; *Brads:* Magic Scraps; *Computer font:* 2Peas Tubby, downloaded from *www.twopeasinabucket.com.*

dad's photos

Supplies *Sticker:* K&Company; *Letter stamps:* Hero Arts and FontWerks; *Stamping ink:* Distress Ink, Ranger Industries; *Photo turn:* Making Memories; *Photo corners:* Canson; *Negative transparency:* Creative Imaginations; *Computer fonts:* Avant Garde Bk BT, Corel WordPerfect; 2Peas Nevermind, downloaded from *www.twopeasinabucket.com*; *Other:* Ribbon, black buckle and brad.

quick idea: Sometimes a single sticker is enough. In fact, I find it almost easier to use one sticker than many. Simply select your favorite.

I have boxes and boxes of my parents' photographs. Not by their choice, granted. I kinda just pirated them. Swore up and down that I'd get them back to them in one piece. And I fully intend to as soon as I'm done copying every last snap shot. Most is your standard fare, only made priceless because it is our history. But every now & again, I run across an incredible gem of a shot. Dad worked magic with that old Nikon 35 mm manual camera. They are photos that I, as a scrapbooker, dream of taking myself because they capture such truth. He has made my job easy for me. I have these (and many other) treasures to work with. Thanks Dad...you did good.

3.
paint
and ink

02 25 05

We were eating dinner and the topic of kids came up. Our kids to be more specific. The ones that, at the moment, are just figments of our imaginations. They've been on our minds lately. Things have been moving in that direction for some time now. I call it sky diving without a parachute. Officially, we're "not NOT trying", if it can be called that. Reminds me of a girl getting a pre-engagement ring. No real commitment, yet a step in the right direction. Flirtatious banter between us now includes a new line..."wanna roll the dice"? Makes you want to roll your eyes instead, doesn't it? Just leaving things up to fate. And we've both been cool with that. Until dinner the other night...

27

Matt hushed up my chatter. Made me put down my slice of pizza. Grabbed my hands across the table and wanted some serious eye contact. Told me he loved me and he was ready to have kids with me. Stopped me in my tracks. What every woman wants to hear from her husband, right? Wow. Oh wow. And then...panic. I'm not ready. Sure, in theory, maybe. But honest to goodness doing something about it...I'm not so decisive. Not really ready for that reality check. Too many things to do. Places to see. Things to experience. Not to mention I'm pretty darn happy just being me at the moment. Oh God. All of a sudden, leaving things up to fate is taking a scary turn.

28

My response was a rather flippant "but it isn't just up to you". Put this girl on the spot and you are bound to get attitude. He knows me well enough to expect it. But, it's black and white as far as he is concerned. I know he isn't changing his mind. He never goes back on things like this. Me...it's all shades of grey. Reasons not to and the reasons to say "heck with it" all blending into each other. He's holding tight to his position. Just waiting for me to catch up with him. That's always been the case with anything; dating, first "I love you's", weddings. Precedence states that I'll catch up shortly. Just a matter of a little time. He's just leading the way. A new chapter is about to begin, it's just up to me to turn the page.

Black & White Shades of Grey

black & white ...: shades of grey

Supplies *Patterned paper:* Sarah Lugg for Colorbök; *Acrylic paint, ribbon charms and rub-ons:* Making Memories; *Computer fonts:* Avant Garde, Corel WordPerfect; 2Peas Tasklist and 2Peas Tubby, downloaded from *www.twopeasinabucket.com.*

chapter three

One of the greatest qualities about paint is that it blends. You have endless palette possibilities with just a few colors—which makes it all the more fun. You can add a variety of shades to your layout by simply using a few colors creatively.

Consider painting a gradient on your next layout. Start with your lightest shade and paint a strip. Add a drop of darker paint to your base paint and paint another strip. Continue adding a drop at a time and painting another strip until your last strip is your darkest color. Even if you cover up a little bit of your background with a photo or journaling (who, me?), you'll get the same effect. The shades of gray in this gradient work well to add symbolism to my layout.

In this chapter, I'll share a variety of ways to use paint as well as stamping ink to add detail, texture and color to your layouts.

dye substitution

Before you go out and invest in any type of scrapbook dyes, poke through your supplies for a set of watercolors. I found I could get the same result by using watercolors on fabric and twill. By using a brush with a water chamber, I could push water through the brush at the same time I was painting on the fabric, resulting in better coverage. It may be a little more time-consuming than using the dyes, but with this method you can find out if you like the look and technique before you buy a new supply.

a boston market

Supplies *Patterned paper:* Marcella by Kay for Target; *Vellum:* The Paper Company; *Letter stamps:* Hero Arts and Ma Vinci's Reliquary; *Stamping ink:* Stampin' Up!; *Tags:* Making Memories; *Watercolors:* Angora, Canson; *Twill letters:* Li'l Davis Designs; *Computer fonts:* CK Artisan, "Creative Clips & Fonts by Becky Higgins" CD, Creating Keepsakes; BellcentNamNum B, Corel WordPerfect; *Other:* Fabric.

CLEVELAND guitars

summer '02

the girl who said boy

erin age 4 e

Once upon a time, there was a little girl. This little girl was cute and playful and super friendly. BUT, she had a little secret. She had trouble saying certain words. Her parents, who were VERY concerned, decided she needed to see a speech therapist. Every week, they piled her and her brother and sister into their Pinto station wagon and drove all the way to Oregon so she could get help saying all those words she couldn't say. One of the words, "boy", was particularly difficult. She would say it "buoy" and although she thought that was perfectly fine, her parents and her speech therapist thought otherwise. They bought her a little blue hand-held mirror. Every night, before she went to bed, she would hold the mirror up and watch her mouth move over the words. She practiced, and practiced, and practiced until she couldn't practice any more. But still, it was just "buoy, buoy, buoy". Finally, after a long time, she was practicing one night and out it popped. BOY! It was as simple as could be. She jumped out of bed and ran to her mother, shouting the word at the top of her lungs for all to hear. Her mom was so proud! And even though she is grown up now, the little girl remembers the day she said "boy" as if it was yesterday. The memory is as crystal clear as her voice saying that one little word.

As for the word "boy", she says it often. Her cats are "silly boys", her husband is her "luv-er boy", and when she gets upset, she tries her best to refrain her language and only say "oh boy!". But don't ask her to say "fuselage". She gave up on that one. I mean, how often are you going to have to say "fuselage"? Not often. That's what I thought!

cleveland guitars

Supplies *Patterned papers and die cuts:* KI Memories; *Foam stamps, acrylic paint and rub-ons:* Making Memories; *Stickers:* Chatterbox; *Button:* Junkitz; *Stamping ink:* ColorBox, Clearsnap.

QUICK IDEA While mixed and matched titles with three-dimensional and letter stickers are popular, you can get a fun and funky look by mixing stamped letters into the title as well. It's a nice touch—especially when you're missing a letter sticker and need to fill the space.

the girl who said boy

Supplies *Patterned papers:* American Crafts; *Letter stamps:* Ma Vinci's Reliquary; *Stamping ink:* Stampin' Up!; *Pen:* Pigment Pro, American Crafts; *Computer font:* Times New Roman, Microsoft Word.

QUICK IDEA Stamps are a perfect way to place letters, titles or journaling into the geometric shapes that are popular on many patterned papers today. If the letter edges don't have quite the crisp image that the graphic paper calls for, simply outline the stamped letters with a matching colored marker.

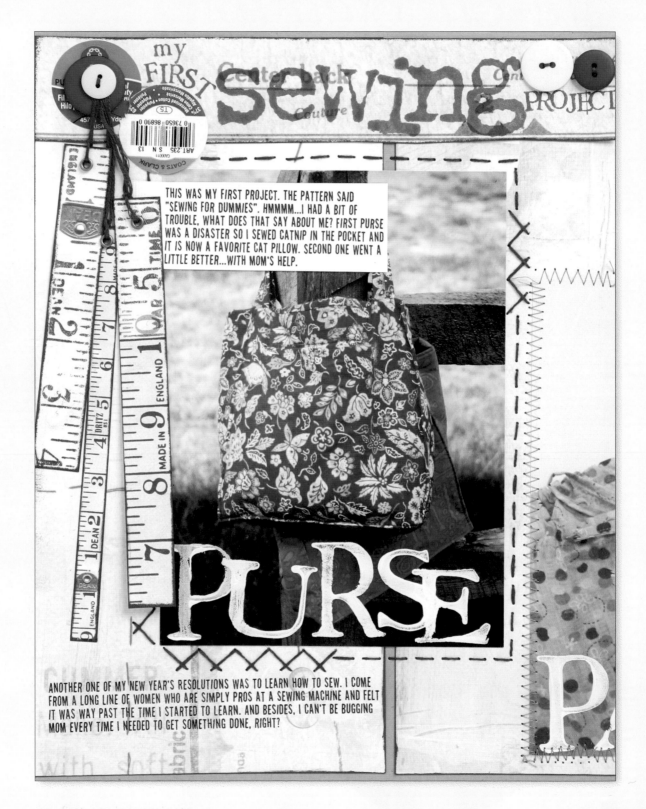

my FIRST sewing PROJECT

THIS WAS MY FIRST PROJECT. THE PATTERN SAID "SEWING FOR DUMMIES". HMMMM...I HAD A BIT OF TROUBLE, WHAT DOES THAT SAY ABOUT ME? FIRST PURSE WAS A DISASTER SO I SEWED CATNIP IN THE POCKET AND IT IS NOW A FAVORITE CAT PILLOW. SECOND ONE WENT A LITTLE BETTER...WITH MOM'S HELP.

PURSE

ANOTHER ONE OF MY NEW YEAR'S RESOLUTIONS WAS TO LEARN HOW TO SEW. I COME FROM A LONG LINE OF WOMEN WHO ARE SIMPLY PROS AT A SEWING MACHINE AND FELT IT WAS WAY PAST THE TIME I STARTED TO LEARN. AND BESIDES, I CAN'T BE BUGGING MOM EVERY TIME I NEEDED TO GET SOMETHING DONE, RIGHT?

my first sewing projects

Supplies *Patterned papers:* Autumn Leaves, Design Originals and 7gypsies; *Foam stamps, acrylic paint and buttons:* Making Memories; *Stamping ink:* Distress Ink, Ranger Industries; *Stitching template:* Li'l Davis Designs; *Computer font:* 2Peas Tasklist, downloaded from *www.twopeasinabucket.com; Other:* Embroidery floss, pins and fabric.

quick idea Don't limit stamped images to cardstock or paper—consider making them a part of your photos. I like this look because it gives each photo a "title," and the stamps become an integral part of the design as well.

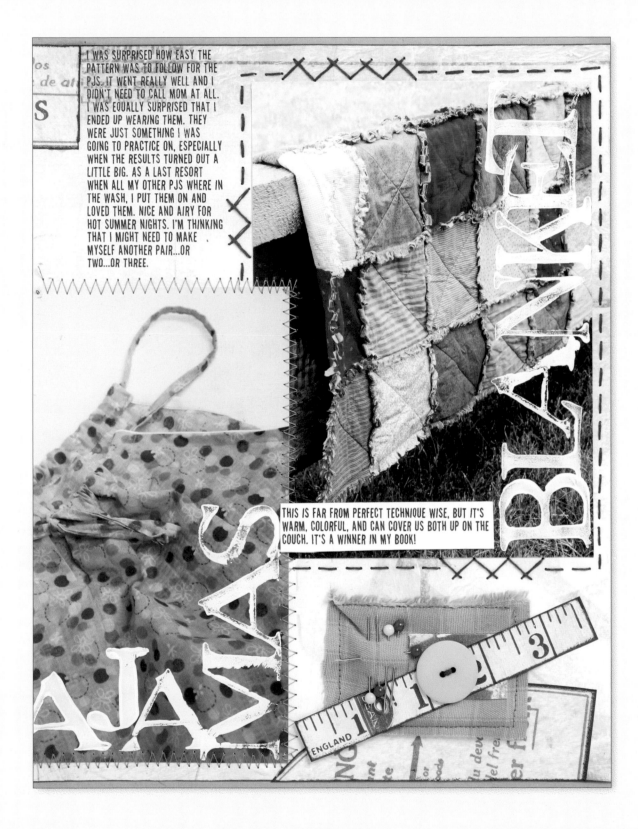

I WAS SURPRISED HOW EASY THE PATTERN WAS TO FOLLOW FOR THE PJS. IT WENT REALLY WELL AND I DIDN'T NEED TO CALL MOM AT ALL. I WAS EQUALLY SURPRISED THAT I ENDED UP WEARING THEM. THEY WERE JUST SOMETHING I WAS GOING TO PRACTICE ON, ESPECIALLY WHEN THE RESULTS TURNED OUT A LITTLE BIG. AS A LAST RESORT WHEN ALL MY OTHER PJS WHERE IN THE WASH, I PUT THEM ON AND LOVED THEM. NICE AND AIRY FOR HOT SUMMER NIGHTS. I'M THINKING THAT I MIGHT NEED TO MAKE MYSELF ANOTHER PAIR...OR TWO...OR THREE.

THIS IS FAR FROM PERFECT TECHNIQUE WISE, BUT IT'S WARM, COLORFUL, AND CAN COVER US BOTH UP ON THE COUCH. IT'S A WINNER IN MY BOOK!

a new look
at templates

Have you ever thought of using your old lettering templates as a stencil? The alphabet is arranged in a unique pattern. When used as a whole, you can make very cool background paper. Here, I simply taped the template on my paper and sprayed it with colorwash. When I removed the template, only the letters remained.

cleveland metropark zoo

Supplies *Patterned paper:* Pebbles Inc.; *Transparency:* Karen Foster Design; *Lettering template:* EK Success; *Elephant template:* Provo Craft; *Letter stamps:* PSX Design; *Stamping ink:* Distress Ink, Ranger Industries; *Rub-ons:* Making Memories, Autumn Leaves and KI Memories; *Snap and woven label:* Making Memories; *Sticker:* K&Company; *Concho:* Scrapworks; *Color wash:* Adirondack Color Wash, Ranger Industries; *Pen:* Zig Writer, EK Success; *Computer font:* 2Peas Tasklist, downloaded from *www.twopeasinabucket.com*; *Other:* Compass button.

snow bunny

Supplies *Patterned papers:* Provo Craft and KI Memories; *Letter stamps:* FontWerks; *Stickers:* SEI; *Snowflake charms, brad, metal-rimmed tag and buttons:* Making Memories; *Acrylic paint:* Delta Technical Coatings; *Snowflake clip and letter conchos:* Scrapworks; *Snaps:* Doodlebug Design; *Embossing powder:* Ranger Industries; *Colored pencils:* Staedtler; *Computer font:* 2Peas Tasklist, downloaded from *www.twopeasinabucket.com*; *Other:* Bleach.

To get nice vivid lettering on dark cardstock, emboss letter stamps on the cardstock and then bleach the inside of the letters. Use colored pencils to shade the bleached area and voilà—pure color!

what a really fun guy

Supplies *Patterned papers:* Pebbles Inc., K&Company, Daisy D's Paper Co. and Close To My Heart; *Stickers:* Sweetwater and Pebbles Inc.; *Die cuts:* Fresh Cuts, EK Success; *Letter stamps:* Ma Vinci's Reliquary; *Acrylic paint, foam stamps, snaps and rub-ons:* Making Memories; *Scoring tool:* Cutter Bee, EK Success; *Computer font:* 2Peas Squish, downloaded from *www.twopeasinabucket.com; Other:* Ribbon.

quick idea: White paint is my best friend—I use it on my scrapbook pages like one uses BIC Wite-Out in the office. Try running a scoring blade through paint and applying it to your project for a messy stitched look. A little white paint can also cover up a little smudged ink, a little dirt and even some improperly transferred rub-ons.

paint and ink medley

Paint or stamping ink. Which to use? Well, why make that decision at all? This patterned paper inspired me to use both of them to create added depth on my layout. First I used a shadow stamp with white ink on red cardstock. I stamped randomly until I had created a pattern I liked. Originally, this is where I envisioned the technique stopping, but I decided I needed a little more depth than the stamping ink would allow. I added some accent areas by brushing some paint on the same shadow stamp and randomly stamping.

DISGRUNTLED

It's February 3rd.

- That darn groundhog saw it's shadow yesterday. Can we get a 2nd opinion?
- The forecast didn't call for snow, but it's accumulated 2 inches already.
- I'm sick of wearing jeans, fleeces, slippers, and flannel pajamas.

...and the Christmas lights are still up!!

Supplies *Acrylic paint and snaps:* Making Memories; *Stamping ink:* Brilliance, Tsukineko; *Punch:* EK Success; *Computer fonts:* CK Corral, "Fresh Fonts" CD, *Creating Keepsakes; Other:* Metal-rimmed tag.

boston's little italy

Supplies *Patterned papers:* 7gypsies and Scenic Route Paper Co.; *Ribbon:* Little Black Dress Designs; *Charm:* K&Company; *Acrylic paint:* Making Memories; *Stamping ink:* StazOn, Tsukineko; *Envelope closures:* Colorbök; *Transparency:* Grafix; *Computer fonts:* Goldmine, downloaded from the Internet; Avant Garde, Corel WordPerfect; *Other:* Labels.

QUICK IDEA Try painting over any type of patterned paper. Apply the paint with a light hand so part of the background image shows through, even if you use dark colors.

JOURNALING

NAPOLI

VELLINO

SICILIA

VENEZIA

BOSTON'S
Little Italy

finding your
inner artist

There are days when I feel like a hobbyist. Days I feel like a designer. And then there are those days when I feel like an artist. I like those days—they're by far my favorite. On these days, I'm almost filled with this need to create, and just the act is satisfying enough without focusing on the end result.

The surest way to bring out my inner artist is to break out the paint. I think it challenges all of my scrapbooking habits. It's drippy and fluid by its very nature, and I can't fight it, even if I try.

I think it's so important to challenge your creativity. Try putting on a different hat and seeing yourself as a different type of artist. It could be paint or a completely different medium that sparks your creativity. The important thing is to stretch yourself and to enjoy the process.

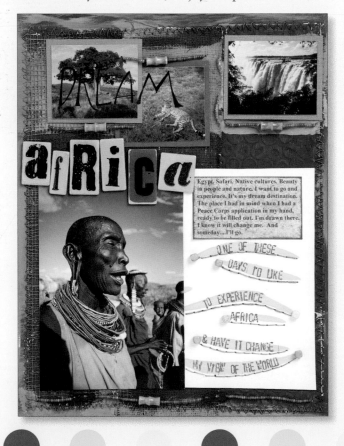

africa

Supplies *Patterned paper:* Provo Craft; *Specialty papers:* Magenta, Creative Imaginations and K&Company; *Acrylic paint, beads, wire and rub-ons:* Making Memories; *Letter stamps:* FontWerks; *Foam stamps:* Canvas Concepts; *Stamping ink:* Stampin' Up!; *Chipboard letters:* Li'l Davis Designs; *Computer font:* Times New Roman, Microsoft Word; *Other:* Embroidery floss and wooden beads.

quick idea: For a unique effect, paint over different paper textures.

The Princess Leonide, sitting on an usurped throne, decides to pay a visit to the sole surviving member of the original royal family. His name is Agis, and one look at his hunky self is all it takes to send Leonide over the moon in love. Unfortunately, he has been most carefully raised by his two guardians, Hermocrate and Leotine, to be scornful of love, hate women, and detest the Princess, whom he has never seen. What's a girl to do? Dress up as a boy and make all three of them fall in love with her, of course.

"I don't demand your love...I crave it!"

After his stunning success playing the Wizard in the "Wizard of Oz", Matt decided to take on the role of Dimas, the crotchety gardener in the "Triumph of Love". Winning both roles gave him some self confidence and made him think he had some potential in areas outside his normal comfort zone. I remember sitting in a booth at the Gingerbread Man, eating french fries, and going over lines with him. For this particular role, he had to shave the top of his head to make it seem like he had more of a receding hair line than he really does...we were worried it wouldn't grow back! And although he'd like to forget, I find the fact he once missed an entrance because he feel asleep backstage to be entirely enduring and entirely Matt.

all the world's a stage

Supplies *Patterned papers:* Scenic Route Paper Co. and Daisy D's Paper Co.; *Metal letters:* EK Success; *Other:* Scrabble letters.

Use an embossing-ink pen to trace the words of your title on text patterned paper. Embossing with thick embossing powder will make the letters stand out and give your title a unique twist.

book signing

Supplies *Patterned paper and tag die cut:* BasicGrey; *Hinge, acrylic paint and brads:* Making Memories; *Letter stamps:* FontWerks; *Stamping ink:* Stampin' Up!; *Computer font:* Times New Roman, Microsoft Word; *Other:* Tassel and craft foam.

quick idea For a unique look, shadow-stamp a journaling block with paint onto your photo. Add graphic tape as lines and write your thoughts with letter stamps.

foam frenzy

Foam sheets are quickly becoming a staple in my scrapbooking arsenal. First and foremost, they are dirt-cheap. Hit a good sale and you can walk out of the store with an apparent fortune in foam for just a few dollars. Second, they're a great way to make your own shadow stamps. Just cut them into your desired shape, apply paint and stamp at will. Another bonus? Your shapes can be reused or cut down for other projects, and if you do need to throw them away, it isn't a big deal because they're so cheap.

A few pointers? If you're using inkpads, as I did on my "Bad Map" layout, lay the foam down and dab it all over with the inkpad. You'll see lines where the edge of your inkpad was on the foam, right? It doesn't look all that even. You can easily solve this problem by using a wet foam paint brush to brush over the foam. This gives the ink some added moisture and evens out the tone, resulting in even coverage when stamped. Also, make sure to flatten your project underneath something heavy, otherwise the paper will warp.

Idea to note: If you're going to make a background or accent using this technique, do it twice. You never know when you might make a mistake, and it's better not to start from scratch.

bad map ... bad!

...the adventure **continues**

Let me start this whole thing out saying it wasn't my fault! Good grief. Can we not read a map? In our defense, the metro stop we were trying to get to in Boston only existed on paper. We found it after a two mile walk from another metro stop and it was under construction. Retrospect, we should have taken this as a sign The restaurant we were trying to find was horrible.

Supplies *Patterned papers:* Daisy D's Paper Co. and Hot Off The Press; *Letter stamps:* FontWerks; *Stamping ink:* Clearsnap and Stampin' Up!; *Chain and eyelet:* Making Memories; *Pen:* Pigment Pro, American Crafts; *Computer fonts:* IowaOldSt BT, downloaded from the Internet; AL Uncle Charles, "Essential Fonts" CD, Autumn Leaves.

I'm not a girl who needs diamonds...or fancy clothes...or roses on Valentine's Day. My **greatest desires** are a little different. I need my bedroom wallpaper stripped. Or a **brick patio** put in the backyard. And a split rail **fence** to grow tendrils of flowers on. Matt pulls through every time and not only puts up with my scheming, but does so happily. I tease him that he just likes wearing the **tool belt** around the house. And any excuse to go to **Home Depot**, we know he's totally down with. But I know he does it for me. **My hardworking man**... making progress and making me happy is all in a hard day's work.

HARD WORKING MAN

THANK YOU

hardworking man

Supplies *Letter stencils:* Autumn Leaves; *Acrylic paint, rub-ons and snaps:* Making Memories; *Walnut ink:* Fiber Scraps; *Index tabs:* 7gypsies; *Charm:* Karen Foster Design; *Embossing powder:* Stampabilities; *Other:* Wire mesh.

quick idea: Use paint to pull all the elements of a layout together. By painting the letter stencils and the metal mesh red, I tied the elements together nicely with the randomly placed red words in the journaling block.

**Like father,
Like son.**

Mr. P. Lincoln...librarian

LHS Connections

Mr. M. Lincoln...Math Dept.

$3x-2y=18$
$+2y=$

MR. LINCOLN

What are the chances? Well, if you ask Mr. Lincoln the statistics teacher, 1 in 10. 10 high schools in the county and Matt just happens to teach at the same one as his Dad. Now retired, Peter was the librarian at Linganore High School for years. When Matt started, everyday he'd walk past the library and the picture of his Dad, hanging above the library door, on his way to his classroom. Some of the more veteran teachers who still work there remember Matt running wild through the halls as a kid. And the principal? Well, Mrs. Lyburn was the VP at Middletown when both Matt and I attended there. I still feel like I should mind my P's and Q's when I see her, even at facility parties. Small world. It's a unique situation. Has the feeling of a torch being passed down. The Lincoln family is full of teachers and Matt is just the latest generation making his mark on young minds...scary, huh?!?!?

FCPS

mr. lincoln

Supplies *Patterned papers:* Rusty Pickle (composition book) and Karen Foster Design (notebook prints); *Apple accent:* Jolee's by You, Sticko for EK Success; *Letter stamps:* Fusion Art Rubber Stamps; *Ribbon:* Bobbin Ribbon; *Stamping ink:* Nick Bantock, Ranger Industries; *Brads:* Karen Foster Design and Making Memories; *Computer fonts:* 2Peas Crate, downloaded from *www.twopeasinabucket.com*; Typist, downloaded from the Internet; *Other:* Bookplates.

QUICK IDEA Want a new twist on a stamped title? Stamp your title with your favorite letter stamps onto cardstock or paper. Cut out a few random letters and back them with cardstock for a varied look.

There was a time before I scrapbooked (shocker!) where I knew I needed an artistic hobby. Something creative. But

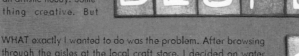

WHAT exactly I wanted to do was the problem. After browsing through the aisles at the local craft store, I decided on water color. It just seemed like something I could fart around with, not take too seriously, and just enjoy. Now, in school, the focus was always math and science. I hadn't taken an art class since

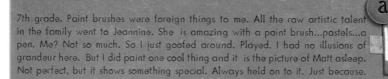

7th grade. Paint brushes were foreign things to me. All the raw artistic talent in the family went to Jeannine. She is amazing with a paint brush...pastels...a pen. Me? Not so much. So I just goofed around. Played. I had no illusions of grandeur here. But I did paint one cool thing and it is the picture of Matt asleep. Not perfect, but it shows something special. Always held on to it. Just because.

desperately seeking a hobby

Supplies *Patterned paper:* BasicGrey; *Letter stamps:* Ma Vinci's Reliquary; *Stamping ink:* ColorBox, Clearsnap; *Stamping ink:* Distress Ink, Ranger Industries; *Metal letter and brads:* Making Memories; *Computer font:* AL Uncle Charles, "Essential Fonts" CD, Autumn Leaves.

quick idea Use a re-inker to create the look of inked "edges" in the middle of a solid sheet of paper. Here's how:
1. Place a couple drops of re-inker on a plastic palette.
2. Using a scrap sheet of paper, dip only the edge into the puddle of re-inker.
3. Take edge of scrap paper, now soaked with re-inker, and touch the edge to the surface of your project. The ink will transfer and will result in an inked-edged look.

painting with a purpose

I came across an advertisement in a magazine that I loved and worked it into the design of this page. It was an ideal fit for some feelings I wanted to express. To show what's truly important to me, I listed many of my favorite things and crossed almost everything out, leaving the most important. I could have used a pen to cross things out (like it seems they did in the ad), but I chose paint instead. I think it's more artsy and it seems more fluid. Paint is a great way to show movement and flow with little effort.

Occasionally, I start playing the worry wort in my head. I'm full of "what if's". What if my iPod stopped working? Or what if the house burned down? What if I didn't have a good job? Silly worries, I realize, but I can't help myself sometimes. The results are good however, because I realize just how lucky and blessed in life I am to have all these things. And I realize that if something does happen, I could deal. Life goes on.

BUT, there are exceptions. There are a few "what if's" that are quickly followed by "I couldn't bear it's" in my head. Always the same thing. I simply would lose my mind if I lost the ones I love. Take away anything else, **ANYTHING!** Make me homeless, make me poor, take away my health just don't take away them. They are my everything. The only things that are truly important.

And so, my only daily prayer is this. The only thing I ask and the only thing I want ... **please just keep them safe.**

PLEASE JUST KEEP THEM SAFE

Family
HOME

IPODS OPRAH CAMERA JEEP
TOWNHOUSE SCRAPBOOKING
READING NICE CLOTHES JOBS
SUMMER VACATIONS EATING
OUT MY LOVED ONES CABLE
INTERNET CELL PHONES ICE
CREAM TIME OFF COMPUTERS
DATES PHOTOGRAPHY MOVIES

The things that are important to me.

Supplies *Patterned paper:* Carolee's Creations; *Stickers and acrylic paint:* Making Memories; *Flower die cuts:* Forget Me Not Designs; *Envelope and punches:* EK Success; *Computer fonts:* 2Peas Tasklist and 2Peas Rickety, downloaded from *www.twopeasinabucket.com;* Times New Roman, Microsoft Word.

sister mary norbert

Supplies *Foam stamps, acrylic paint and metal plaque:* Making Memories; *Leaf rubber stamp:* Trading Spaces, Canvas Concepts; *Embossing powder:* Ultra Thick Embossing Enamel, Ranger Industries; *Stamping ink:* Ranger Industries; *Big brads:* Karen Foster Design; *Computer fonts:* Avant Garde Bk BT, Corel WordPerfect; Stamp Act, downloaded from the Internet; Times New Roman, Microsoft Word.

quick idea: To double the number of foam stamps you own, simply use the backside of the stamp as a shadow stamp. I used both sides of a medallion stamp to create the background on the right-hand side of this layout. Use the edges when pushing down to avoid ruining the delicate stamp.

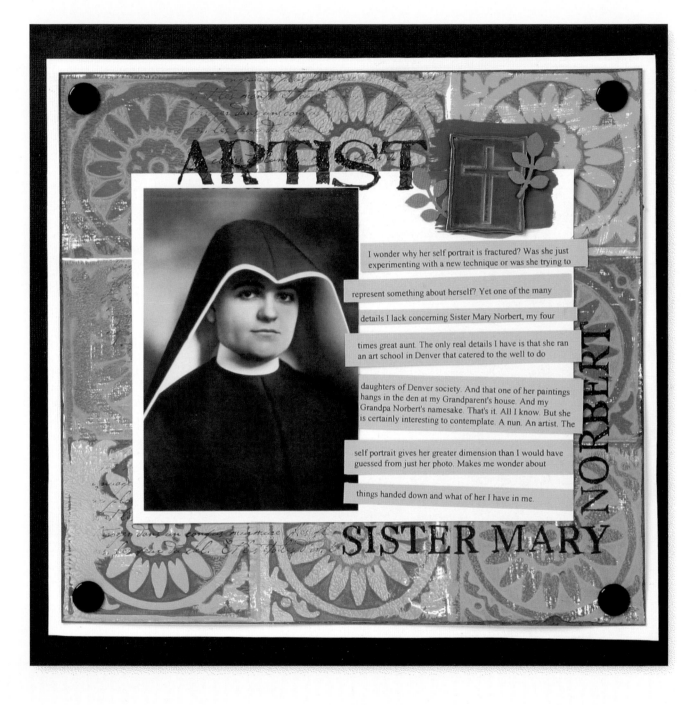

ARTIST

I wonder why her self portrait is fractured? Was she just experimenting with a new technique or was she trying to

represent something about herself? Yet one of the many

details I lack concerning Sister Mary Norbert, my four

times great aunt. The only real details I have is that she ran an art school in Denver that catered to the well to do

daughters of Denver society. And that one of her paintings hangs in the den at my Grandparent's house. And my Grandpa Norbert's namesake. That's it. All I know. But she is certainly interesting to contemplate. A nun. An artist. The

self portrait gives her greater dimension than I would have guessed from just her photo. Makes me wonder about

things handed down and what of her I have in me.

SISTER MARY NORBERT

4.

craft embellishments

Then: My lace collar itched. The bows & ruffles made me look like a baby. I wish it could be store bought. And horrors of all horrors, I matched my little sister.
Now: I can't get over how adorable we looked...so very appropriate for little girls. Mom showed her love in stitches and calico and matching outfits. How lucky was I?
Spring 1985
Spring 1982
Mom always made our clothes. At the time, I didn't appreciate it. But now I realize how special it was.
Centro de la parte de atrás
Center
Homemade
DRESSES
Christmas 1982
Christmas 1987
Spring 1984

homemade dresses

Supplies *Patterned papers:* Daisy D's Paper Co., Sweetwater, Design Originals, K&Company and me & my BIG ideas; *Stitching template:* Li'l Davis Designs; *Date stamp:* Making Memories; *Stamping ink:* Stampin' Up!; *Punch:* Emagination Crafts; *Computer fonts:* CK Windsong, "Creative Clips & Fonts by Becky Higgins" CD, *Creating Keepsakes;* Times New Roman, Microsoft Word; *Other:* Letter beads, embriodery floss, buttons and slides.

chapter four

Then: My lace collar itched. The bows and ruffles made me look like a baby. I wished it could be store-bought. And horror of all horrors, I matched my little sister.

Now: I can't get over how adorable we looked ... so very appropriate for little girls. Mom showed her love in stitches and calico and matching outfits. How lucky was I?

With Mom's talent for sewing and my early exposure to fabric, thread, eyelet lace, buttons and more, how could I resist not transferring items from the sewing world onto my personal scrapbook pages? As a matter of fact, how can I resist transferring items from the office supply store or the hardware store or that cute little gift shop down the block? I'll admit it: I can't.

Embellishments help tell the story on your layouts. And, in this chapter, I'll show you all kinds of different embellishments as well as lots of unique looks you can create with them.

a whole package of product

Occasionally, I just go hog wild and use almost a whole package of something on just one layout. For my Beanie Baby layout (don't laugh!), I used a whole package of circular slide holders. I placed the photographs in different positions and covered the slide holders with different types of paper. The consistency of the circles helps unify the layout and gives it a fun feel.

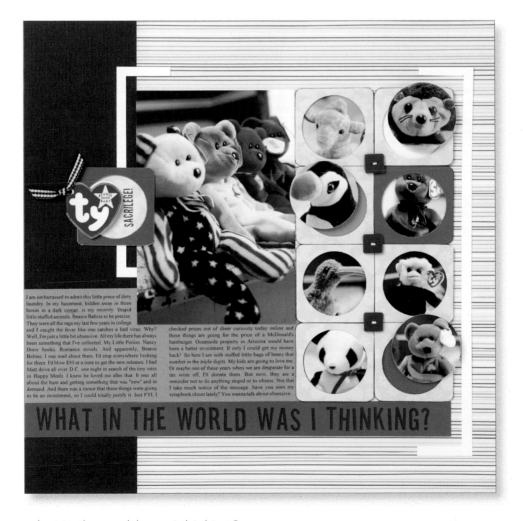

what in the world was i thinking?

Supplies *Patterned paper:* KI Memories; *Buttons:* Making Memories; *Circular slide holders:* Hot Off The Press; *Pop dots:* All Night Media; *Computer fonts:* 2Peas Tasklist, downloaded from *www.twopeasinabucket.com*; Times New Roman, Microsoft Word; *Other:* Ribbon.

Never, ever, ever have we worked so hard. Matt's 1st season doing taxes in his mother's office coincided almost perfectly with the bulk of my book work. Alone, it would have been fine, but our "real" jobs on top of it all has made things very intense for the last few months. I joked after our brief hiatus at Xmas that I understood why people can have nervous breakdowns. I think both of us, at one time or another, have wished it would all go away. But we've sucked it up and we are almost there. The thing that has got us through? The thought of summer. Relaxing on the patio with a book and a beer. How many times have we mentioned that scenario? More than I can count. Soon, Babe, oh so soon. We've earned it.

Scrapbooks + Research + Taxes + Teaching = 2 Busy People

This is exactly how Matt's childhood friend described him once. The little boy with the big vocabulary. I keep asking just what types of words he used to use, but they have long been forgotten. Patrice just says that he was always very articulate and well spoken. Petrie says he still is. Matt will tell you that his parents never talked to him like a child, but rather an adult with real conversations, and he just picked it up from there.

One of my favorite stories is about the time Matt was being bullied in the boy's restroom. Not a stretch...he was a little nerdy. The only way I can get away with saying that is because I was right there with him in the land of nerdom. Instead of relying on what muscle he had to defend himself, Matt let out this minute long litany of inventive name calling and curse words (gasp!) that left Mr. Bully standing there with his mouth hanging open in shock. Matt walked out victorious and unscathed. That's my guy. Slaying 'em with words. A small victory for nerds everywhere.

the kid who talks like an old man

Quote by Eric Thomas

second shift

Supplies *Patterned papers:* SEI, Chatterbox and KI Memories; *Alphabet buttons:* Junkitz; *Rivets:* Chatterbox; *Punch:* EK Success; *Computer fonts:* Times New Roman, Microsoft Word; 2Peas Tubby, downloaded from *www.two-peasinabucket.com.*

quick idea: I used alphabet buttons to create the look of a clock on my page.

the kid who talks like an old man

Supplies *Patterned paper:* Scrapworks; *Rub-ons and mini eyelets:* Making Memories; *Buttons:* American Crafts; *Computer fonts:* Times New Roman, Microsoft Word; CK Windsong, "Creative Clips & Fonts by Becky Higgins" CD, Creating Keepsakes; *Other:* Ribbon.

quick idea: Did I mention that I love buttons? Here, I turned them into a unique page border by threading them differently and attaching them on top of and underneath cardstock circles.

fiber creativity

Fiber. I'll admit it. I bought tons of it when it was so popular three years ago. And, I know there's a good chance you have just as much fiber in your scrapbooking stash as I do. If you've got enough fiber to knit two dozen sweaters, just sit down and play with it and see what kind of accents you can create.

Here are two fun fiber accents I created by playing around with supplies from my stash.

First, the card. The vase on my flower card? That's the result of me just playing around with fiber and a piece of chipboard. I ended up with a cute vase for a nice card (and who can't use more cards?). There's a fun thought for you. Go ahead and experiment with your scrapbook supplies. Even if you don't create something you deem "page-worthy," you might just invent a pretty homemade card.

Second, the layout. My fiber accent looks a bit like one of those bouclé jackets that are popular right now. I like it so much that I'm cooking up new variations as we speak. When I originally created this accent, it had a purple border all the way around it. It reminded me a little too much of a potholder. It had to go. This type of experimentation is all just part of the process.

summer card

Supplies *Watch crystals:* Scrapworks; *Page pebbles:* Making Memories; *Fiber:* Rubba Dub Dub; *Chipboard piece:* Bazzill Basics Paper; *Punch:* EK Success; *Ribbon:* Textured Trios, Michaels; *Computer fonts:* AL Serenade, "Script" CD, Autumn Leaves; Georgia, Microsoft Word.

she likes

PRETTY THINGS

Mom was trying to find a decorating mag for me to see the other day and was having trouble locating it in the piles of old magazines she seems to have archived in my former bedroom. I told her she should rip out her favorite ideas and save them in a notebook. She just laughed. Told me she'd have to rip out the entire magazine. So many good ideas. And the house reflects it. Everything is pretty. Antiques all over. Homemade curtains that look ten fold better than store bought. Colored glass plates stacked for display in the hutch. Flowers in watering cans...old washing machines... ...birdhouses. Flowers everywhere for that matter. So very home for all of us. And so very Mom.

MOM

she likes pretty things

Supplies *Stickers and flowers:* Making Memories; *Letter stamps:* Hero Arts; *Stamping ink:* Stampin' Up!; *Metal buttons:* K&Company; *Fibers:* Rubba Dub Dub and Making Memories; *Other:* Bookplate and brads.

The woven ribbon background includes the following phrases:

- Nor conceited
- Envies no one
- Never boastful
- Kind
- Patient
- Delights in truth
- Matt and Erin
- Does not gloat
- Keeps no score of wrongs
- Never selfish, not quick to take offense

love is

love is

Supplies *Vellum:* Paper Adventures; *Flowers, snaps, brads and rub-ons:* Making Memories; *Bookplate:* Li'l Davis Designs; *Embossing powder:* Ranger Industries; *Computer font:* AL Uncle Charles, "Essential Fonts" CD, Autumn Leaves; *Other:* Ribbon.

quick idea: Weave a ribbon background for a truly elegant look on your page. Use a thick piece of chipboard as your ribbon bases (regular cardstock will bend).

got ribbon ?

I found the ultimate score one day while I was antiquing. Can you believe it? Yards and yards of antique ribbon for just pennies. I bought it all up and haven't regretted the purchase one little bit. It's both gorgeous and versatile, as you can see here.

On this page, I cut evenly placed slits into my cardstock and threaded the ribbon through the slits, alternating colors. I secured each strip of ribbon by adhering it to the back of my layout. And notice how I also criss-crossed ribbon on my page and slipped the ribbon through a pretty ribbon charm.

me & murphy

Supplies *Frame:* My Mind's Eye; *Ribbon charm, heart eyelet and ribbon word:* Making Memories; *Computer fonts:* CityDlig and Georgia, Corel WordPerfect; *Other:* Antique ribbon.

how to make fabric accents

I love adding fabric accents to my layouts. Here are two easy ways to incorporate your favorite fabric pieces to make page accents.

fabric shape accents (see "ruthie" on pg. 101)

1. Punch a shape out of cardstock.
2. Run the shape through a Xyron machine (one side will be coated with adhesive).
3. Place the shape on the back of fabric and cut out.
4. Remove the punched shape. You can use it again to cut out multiple shapes.
5. Roll the fabric shape between your hands to fray it a bit.
6. Place the fabric shape on your page.

fabric letter accents (see "love" on pg. 101)

1. Print your title on paper.
2. Cut the title out.
3. Run it through a Xyron machine.
4. Place the title on the back of your fabric and cut out.
5. Do NOT remove the paper. This will give you a more polished look than the worn flowers on my "Ruthie" layout.
6. Adhere the title to the layout.
7. If you're feeling very patient, stitch your title to the page with a sewing machine. If not, no problem; it will look great as is.

ruthie

Supplies *Letter stamps:* Stampin' Up!; *Tags:* DieCuts with a View; *Buttons:* Junkitz; *Eyelets:* Making Memories; *Punches:* EK Success and Emagination Crafts; *Embossing powder:* Stampabilities; *Conchos:* Scrapworks; *Computer fonts:* Times New Roman and Georgia, Microsoft Word; *Other:* Fabric.

love

Supplies *Patterned papers:* Mustard Moon and Patchwork Paper Design; *Letter stamps:* PSX Design; *Stamping ink:* Stampin' Up!; *Photo corners:* Canson; *Punch:* EK Success; *Computer fonts:* 2Peas Squish, downloaded from www.twopeasinabucket.com; EngravrsRoman BT, Corel WordPerfect; *Other:* Trim, ribbon, antique buttons and fabric.

creative supply substitution

I love mini books. One of the things I think is really cool about them? All the little treasures don't always dwell inside the pages. Little trinkets hanging off the binding, embellishments adorning the front cover and items poking off the edges add a cool funkiness to the design that helps transform it from "just" an album to a piece of art.

I wanted to add tabs to this little mini "Summer" book and decided to use buttons. I was actually able to stamp words on the buttons with a mini stamp set and solvent ink. I love the look of the colorful button tabs.

The next time you sit down to work on a layout, think about making a creative substitution on your page. Instead of tabs, try buttons. Instead of a ribbon, try a strip of crinkled paper. Instead of a photo turn, try a paper clip. The possibilities are endless—and it's a great way to be creative in your scrapbooking as well as tap into supplies you think you might never use again. The results will be unique and totally you.

summer mini album
Supplies *Patterned papers:* Chatterbox; *Chipboard album:* Li'l Davis Designs; *Acrylic paint, button, foam stamps, metal flower and mini page pebbles:* Making Memories; *Letter stamps:* FontWerks and PSX Design; *Stamping ink:* Tsukineko and Stampin' Up!.

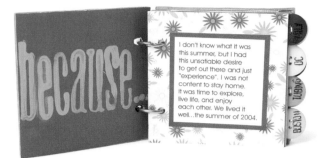

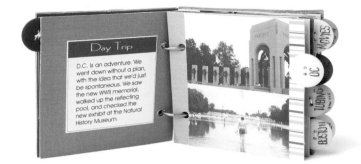

because

I don't know what it was this summer, but I had this unsatiable desire to get out there and just "experience". I was not content to stay home. It was time to explore, live life, and enjoy each other. We lived it well...the summer of 2004.

Day Trip

D.C. is an adventure. We went down without a plan, with the idea that we'd just be spontaneous. We saw the new WWII memorial, walked up the reflecting pool, and checked the new exhibit at the Natural History Museum.

Baker Park

I hope they do this every summer! Movies in the park on Saturday nights. I went with Liz and Danny to see "Grease" in June and then with Matt and his school friends to see "ET" toward the end of the season. Again, we just enjoyed being a part of the community. I love Frederick!

Vacation for 2

Before we joined the family in NH at the lake, we flew into Boston and spent a few days by ourselves. Lots of walking and exploring, which is what we like to do best. Our favorite thing was Little Italy... the food was AMAZING!

Charlestown, WV

We finally got around to doing this! It was a little rainy, but we didn't let that slow us down. I though it was so sweet that Matt went to the bank and got us two dollar bills to make our bets. That was thinking ahead!

Firecracker 5K

I loved that my family came out to support me in my run. It just meant so much to have them running by my side. I hope this will evolve into something we do together every year. Of course, that means I need to get back to running so I can be ready!

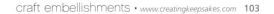

poker

Supplies *Patterned papers:* Chatterbox and Mustard Moon; *Eyelet word:* Making Memories; *Computer fonts:* 2Peas Tubby and 2Peas Tasklist, downloaded from *www.twopeasinabucket.com*; BauerBodni Blk and Avant Garde, Corel WordPerfect; *Other:* Poker chips, playing cards and magnet strips.

quick idea: Do you have specific products you bought for a particular page? I took the poker pictures in May, bought the poker embellishments in September and didn't finish the layout until February. Challenge yourself to use page-specific products within a certain amount of time and free up your stash for new stuff.

dr*ie*d fl*ow*ers

Dried flowers. Sigh. So pretty. So feminine. So darn delicate I'm

afraid to put them in my scrapbook. Page protectors can only do so

much. So what's a girl to do? The answer is what I like to call "flower

armor." I drizzled dried flowers with clear, thick liquid adhesive and then

carefully covered the flowers with clear epoxy tags (I stamped them first with a

solvent ink to create the "Dad" portion of my title). Gotta love it when things are

pretty and practical at the same time.

dad & daughter

Supplies *Embossed paper:* K&Company; *Letter stamps:* Ma Vinci's Reliquary; *Stamping ink:* StazOn, Tsukineko; *Epoxy tags:* Creative Imaginations; *Rub-ons:* Making Memories; *Ribbon:* Michaels; *Flowers:* Pressed Petals; *Computer fonts:* 2Peas Tubby, downloaded from *www.two-peasinabucket.com*; Times New Roman, Microsoft Word.

supply inspiration

A Vegas page just begs for a little bit of glitter, don't you think? It's contained in a little pocket that makes up the larger color-blocked design on my layout. Just a little layout "bling bling" without being too messy. I smile every time I see it.

Do you have supplies you think you'll never use again? Take those supplies out and do a little brainstorming. Ask yourself what type of page might get you to use it. Take glitter, for example. Glitter reminds me of magic fairies, Las Vegas and little girls. Am I ever going to have pages that will have those themes? Well, I'm hoping there's a little girl in my future, and magic and fairies will naturally follow, so I'm going to hold on to it.

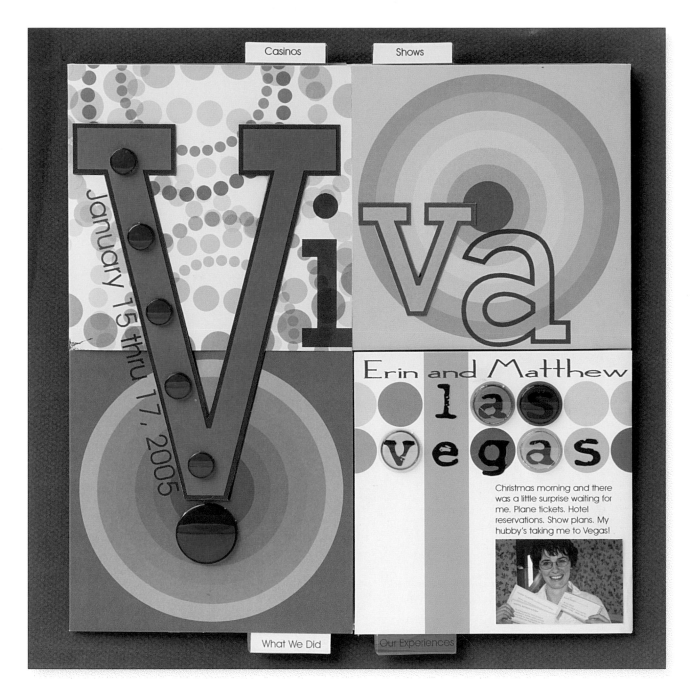

Casinos   Shows

January 15 thru 17, 2005

Erin and Matthew

Christmas morning and there was a little surprise waiting for me. Plane tickets. Hotel reservations. Show plans. My hubby's taking me to Vegas!

What We Did   Our Experiences

viva las vegas

Supplies *Patterned papers, cardstock and cards:* American Crafts; *Stickers:* Creative Imaginations; *Watch crystals:* KI Memories; *Opalescent flakes:* Shaved Ice, Magic Scraps; *Computer fonts:* 2Peas Squish and 2Peas Samantha, downloaded from *www.twopeasinabucket.com;* Avant Garde and GeoS1b712 Md BT, Corel WordPerfect; *Other:* Ribbon and magnet strips.

shabu shabu

Supplies *Patterned paper:* me & my BIG ideas; *Specialty paper:* Paper Garden; *Chopsticks, tags and charms:* Boxer Scrapbook Productions; *Stickers:* Creative Imaginations; *Paper ribbon and acrylic paint:* Making Memories; *Embossing powder:* Ranger Industries; *Computer fonts:* Times New Roman, Microsoft Word; Tiger Rag, downloaded from the Internet.

quick idea: No reason to limit the embellishments you use on your layouts. Look for those perfectly unique touches that really do help tell the story on your page.

After a bit of sightseeing, Todd and Robin took me to this FABULOUS Japanese restaurant in the Kodak Theater complex. *Shabu shabu* is Japanese fondue and I ordered a tiger shrimp and beef plate. To cook it, I just had to throw the thin little pieces of meat, veggies, and noodles in the boiling pot at my seat and seconds later, toss them down with a little soy sauce! I gave a try at the chop sticks, but proved myself to be completely inept. When I asked for real silverware, the server wouldn't let me give up and gave me "cheater" chopsticks instead. I couldn't believe how reasonable the meal was for Southern CA...only $12.99. I had enough left over for my first cosmopolitan AND an apple martini! I guess you could say I had a really good time and thanks to my cell phone, gave Matt a few updates of the experience.

5.
metal
accents

To the outside world we will grow old. But not to brothers and sisters. We know each other as we always were. We know each other's hearts. We

share private family jokes. We remember family feuds and secrets, family griefs and joys. We live outside the touch of time. Clara Ortega

THE THREE OTHER THAN ME

the three other than me

Supplies *Patterned papers:* KI Memories; *Ribbon:* C.M. Offray & Son; *Metal letter stencils:* Colorbök; *Tags:* Making Memories; *Letter stamps:* Hero Arts; *Stamping ink:* Stampin' Up!; *Computer fonts:* 2Peas Tubby, downloaded from *www.twopeasinabucket.com*; AL Meaningful, "Handwritten Fonts" CD, Autumn Leaves.

chapter five

Flashback to the summer of 2002 ... the June issue of *Creating Keepsakes* had a double-page ad from Making Memories. Only, all the pictures were blurred out of the ad so you couldn't see what the new releases were going to be. I could not wait to find out about the new line and even dragged my husband right into a Michaels store (so, yeah, we were on vacation) to find out. I remember the moment I opened the July issue and saw the debut of the Making Memories metal line. Oh! Eyelets in a rainbow of colors ... colored snaps ... alphabet charms ... metal shapes. It was heaven.

That was just the tip of the iceberg for the metal trend. There are now seemingly endless variations of metal letter accents for your scrapbook pages. I love using metal—in small doses (see how I've threaded ribbon through metal circles and backed metal stencils with cardstock on this layout?). I'll admit it: I've got a sizeable stash of metal accents in my scrapbooking closets. Old or new, just a little can be the perfect touch.

In this chapter, I hope you'll be inspired to add that perfect little touch of metal to your pages.

beaded staples

I wanted a pretty, feminine look for this page, and I knew I wanted to do something different. Something with pretty beads, perhaps. But how to string them? I found a surprising answer in my staples. Yep, those little beaded accents on my title? Beaded staples. Here's how you can create a similar accent:

1. Discharge staples from a stapler without bending the prongs.
2. Dab the tips of the prongs on an inkpad.
3. Gently and with a light hand, touch the tips of the inked prongs onto the desired place on your scrapbook page.
4. Use a paper piercer to poke holes on the page where your staple left marks.
5. Unbend one end of the staple (it should look like an "L" as opposed to a "U") and string a few seed beads on the staple.
6. Bend back the one prong and poke through the holes.
7. Flip the page over and bend the prongs to hold the staple in place.

A FREE SPIRIT
One to forge her own path
DANCES TO HER OWN TUNE
Always does her own thing
ORIGINAL

Which is why when Mom first heard the lyrics to "Why Walk When You can Fly?" by Mary Chapin Carpenter, she immediately thought of Jeannine.

WHY WALK WHEN YOU CAN FLY?

why walk when you can fly?

Supplies *Patterned papers:* K&Company and SEI; *Vellum and sticker:* K&Company; *Stamping ink:* Ranger Industries; *Stick pin:* EK Success; *Computer font:* CK Regal, "Creative Clips & Fonts for Special Occasions" CD, *Creating Keepsakes; Other:* Rubber stamp, staples, ribbon and seed beads.

hollywood

Supplies *Patterned paper and stickers:* Karen Foster Design; *Hollywood sign:* Jolee's Boutique, Sticko for EK Success; *Stamping ink:* Ranger Industries; *Computer font:* 2Peas Tubby, downloaded from *www.twopeasinabucket.com*; *Other:* Ribbon, negative strip and charm.

quick idea: A great example of how just one little metal accent can help finish off a title or journaling block on your page.

birthday suit swim

Supplies *Patterned papers:* Paperfever and Mara-Mi; *Jump rings:* Junkitz; *Vellum tags:* Making Memories; *Snaps:* Doodlebug Design; *Computer fonts:* Times New Roman and Georgia, Microsoft Word; 2Peas Tubby, downloaded from *www.twopeasinabucket.com*; *Other:* Embroidery floss.

quick idea: When I discovered these metal jump rings, I knew they'd be the perfect circular design element for my layout. Instead of hanging something from them, I decided to thread string through them. It makes a terrific page border.

FOLLOW THAT CAR

wanderlust

Supplies *Patterned papers:* Creative Imaginations, Chatterbox and K&Company; *Metal button:* K&Company; *Letter stamps:* FontWerks; *Stamping ink:* Stampin' Up!; *Computer fonts:* Times New Roman, Microsoft Word; Cooper BD Mt, Corel WordPerfect; *Other:* Brads and paper clips.

quick idea: Very cheap, very easy. Yep, those are paper clips poking out from behind the photo of my mom and dad. I just put brads inside each clip to create a whole new look.

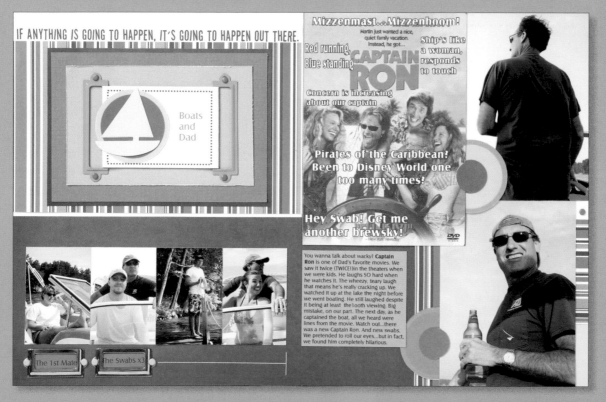

boats and dad

Supplies *Patterned paper:* Designs by Reminisce; *Vellum:* American Crafts; *Bookplates:* Jo-Ann Crafts; *Rub-ons:* KI Memories; *Punch:* Emagination Crafts; *Brads:* Making Memories; *Computer fonts:* 2Peas Tasklist, downloaded from www.twopeasinabucket.com; Times New Roman, Microsoft Word.

quick idea: Notice how I stretched my title between two bookplates? And check it out—I actually finished off my title with a sailboat punch.

hinged layout

Gotta love my cat, even if his behavior isn't as adorable as he is. To create this hinged layout, I attached an extra piece of cardstock to the bottom layer of my spread. The back page slips inside the sheet protector, while the top piece can be lifted to reveal more journaling and photographs.

sure, he looks all sweet & innocent

Supplies *Patterned papers:* SEI, Flair Designs and Mustard Moon; *Vellum:* SEI; *Rub-ons:* KI Memories and Making Memories; *Bookplate:* K&Company; *Photo turns:* 7gypsies; *Hinges:* Making Memories; *Computer fonts:* Unknown.

Aren't we just too cute? One pink bunny suit for all of us. Mom certainly got her money's worth out of this one. Even Skeeter, the lone boy, was not spared from all this cuteness. Just another piece of our shared history.

bunny suit

Supplies *Patterned papers:* Keeping Memories Alive, Anna Griffin, me & my BIG ideas and K&Company; *Letter stamps:* My Sentiments Exactly; *Stamping ink:* Stampin' Up!; *Die cut:* Anna Griffin; *Photo corners:* Making Memories.

quick idea: Here's a tip: Metal has color and visual weight, which needs to be balanced on a page. I've found that using a sheet of dark-gray cardstock serves this purpose well. Notice how the gray photo mats balance out the metal corners at the top of the page.

dorm life

Supplies *Patterned paper:* Scrappin' Dreams; *Clips and snaps:* Making Memories; *Punch:* EK Success; *Computer fonts:* Avant Garde, Corel WordPerfect; CK Windsong, "Creative Clips & Fonts by Becky Higgins" CD, *Creating Keepsakes.*

quick idea: It's fun to experiment with paper clips. Here, I placed cute little snaps inside the clips, joined them together and added them to the page.

Elizabeth's first semester at UMBC, 9/03

charmed, *i*'m sure

As a child, I loved my collection of little plastic necklaces. After a dozen or more trips to the Hallmark store to choose charms that held some sort of significance to me, I was decked out in true 80s style. I decided to use charms the same way on this layout. The ones I chose reflect the holidays and events depicted on the layout. A ribbon with jump ring "connectors" helps complete the look.

MOM What do you want for **CHRISTMAS?** **YOUR BIRTHDAY?** **MOTHER'S DAY?** **YOUR ANNIVERSARY?**

"I JUST WANT YOU ALL TO GET ALONG!"

i just want you all to get along

Supplies *Patterned paper:* Marcella by Kay for Target; *Jump rings and eyelet charms:* Making Memories; *Ribbon:* C.M. Offray & Son; *Computer font:* Avant Garde, Corel WordPerfect; *Other:* Charms.

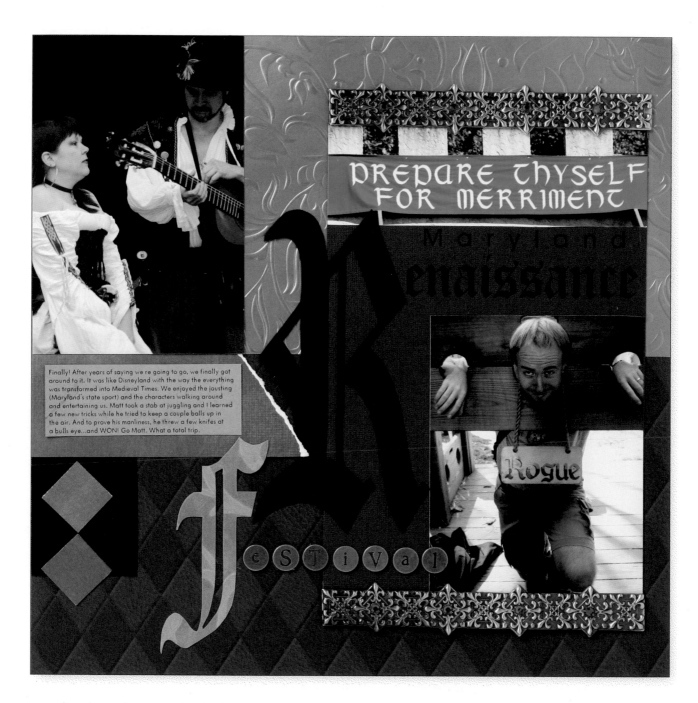

maryland renaissance festival

Supplies *Patterned papers:* K&Company and Scenic Route Paper Co.; *Specialty paper:* K&Company; *Metal letters:* Making Memories; *Metal border embellishments:* EK Success; *Ribbon:* C.M. Offray & Son; *Computer fonts:* Cloisterblack BT, Corel WordPerfect; AL Uncle Charles, "Essential Fonts" CD, Autumn Leaves; *Other:* Rhinestones.

quick idea: These pewter border accents from EK Success were the perfect complement to this layout. I wanted to create a bit more of a medieval look, so I added just a few rhinestones.

Some people really get into it this whole thing. I can't tell you how many times I got called "m'lady". We contemplated renting costumes, but opted to play it cool instead. And besides, I don't think I could have handled the low necked tops all the women were wearing...I'll keep my boobs to myself, thanks. One of the things that really made me smile, however was all the families that were there all decked out. What a great thing to do with kids.

OMG. The food. I really think the main reason people go is just for the food. You name it, they had it...right down to fried pickles and turkey legs. I give you one guess which one of those I enjoyed. Pickles? YUCK! Every where we turned there was something new to sample. I was in heaven...they had hard cider on tap. Matt tried the mead wine. It was a little too sweet for me when I used it to wash down that hunk of turkey meat.

packing-tape transfer on metal

I wanted to get a little funky on this CD holder and was inspired to try something I'd never tried before: a packing-tape transfer. See the red "movies" background on the metal tin? I transferred the image using packing tape, and I love the way it turned out.

How to do a packing-tape transfer:

1. Make a photocopy of the design you would like to transfer. (I created my document in Microsoft Word, printed it and photo copied it on a copy machine. You cannot transfer something printed from a bubble-jet or ink-jet printer. The toner just doesn't allow for it—I learned this the hard way!)

2. Press the packing tape down on your photocopy. Yep, stick it right to the image. You will transfer whatever is on the sticky part of the tape.
   Note: If your surface is larger than the width of your tape, you need to lay it on the transfer with the edges lining up ... like applying wallpaper.

3. Use the back of a spoon to rub the tape over the image (you want it to stick really well).

4. Soak the taped image in a bowl of warm water for several minutes. Using your fingers, gently rub the paper away from the packing tape. The paper will rub off, but the image will remain on the tape.

5. Place the packing-tape image wherever you'd like it to be. It might be sticky enough to stay in place on its own, or you might need to attach it with a clear sealer.

favorite movies

Supplies *Patterned papers and stickers:* Karen Foster Design; *Tin:* Boxer Scrapbook Productions; *Metal stencils and colored conchos:* Scrapworks; *Eyelet charm, snap, beaded chain and eyelets:* Making Memories; *Punch:* Fiskars; *Computer fonts:* Times New Roman, Microsoft Word; Compata Lt Bt, Corel WordPerfect; CK Chemistry, "Fresh Fonts" CD, *Creating Keepsakes; Other:* Packing tape and movie images.

fireworks

Supplies *Patterned papers:* Daisy D's Paper Co., Chatterbox and Provo Craft; *Stickers, ribbon and metal-rimmed tags:* Making Memories; *Rub-ons:* Autumn Leaves and Making Memories; *Jump rings:* Junkitz; *Epoxy stickers:* Creative Imaginations; *Computer fonts:* Times New Roman, Microsoft Word; CK Stenography, "Fresh Fonts" CD, *Creating Keepsakes.*

quick idea: I layered three epoxy stickers for a dimensional page title. I included a different element with each layer. Notice the patterned paper, rub-ons and stickers? A metal tag rim rounds the edges and completes the look.

creative substitutions

Sometimes, traditional stitching on a layout is too much of a feminine look. But sometimes I think a layout needs stitching to look finished. What to do, what to do? This is the dilemma that most often inspires new ideas for me. A problem that needs a solution. Substituting one thing for another. Finding a replacement to meet my vision. This for that. It works just about every time for me.

This time? Well, I had this zipper I didn't know what to do with. Taking it apart and just allowing the zipper teeth to poke out resulted in a more masculine substitute for machine-stitching. My men wouldn't have settled for anything girlie.

flying lessons

Supplies *Patterned paper, tags and tacks:* Chatterbox; *Vellum:* American Crafts; *Buckles:* KI Memories; *Lettering template:* Pebbles for EK Success; *Zipper:* Junkitz; *Pens:* Zig Scroll & Brush, EK Success; Pigment Pro, American Crafts; *Metal chain:* Making Memories; *Computer fonts:* CK Chemistry, "Fresh Fonts" CD, *Creating Keepsakes*; 2Peas Tubby, downloaded from www.twopeasinabucket.com.

...SAY YEA!

I don't know what happened exactly, but I've suddenly developed an opinion in politics. What was once complete apathy has morphed into a need to have my voice be counted. Perhaps I have

Pro Gun Control

Pro Gay Rights

VO TE

Reduce the Deficit

Pro Civil Liberties

seen what a privilege it is to cast a ballot. As a woman, as a person, as a member of society. People have died to give me this right. So, with that thought, I voted for the first time.

VOTE

MAKE

A STAND

ALL IN FAVOR

Vote

Supplies *Patterned papers:* Making Memories and Doodlebug Design; *Mailbox letters, stickers and rub-on letters:* Making Memories; *Punch:* McGill; *Tabs:* Avery; *Computer font:* Avant Garde, Corel WordPerfect; *Other:* Magnetic strip.

quick idea: **Need a fun little way to use mailbox letters?** Turn them into interactive elements for a fun surprise on your page.

Bottom line...my values should not be able to dictate what others can and cannot do. We all have different beliefs and points of view. Why force yours on others? Tolerance, all around.

04'

CAST YOUR BALLOT

A DIFFERENCE TAKE

BE HEARD...VOTE!

kid sister

Supplies *Patterned paper:* Paperfever and Mustard Moon; *Metal charms, anchors and brads:* Making Memories; *Rub-ons:* KI Memories; *Button:* American Crafts; *Rickrack:* C.M. Offray & Son; *Computer fonts:* CK Regal, "Creative Clips & Fonts for Special Occasions" CD, *Creating Keepsakes;* 2Peas Roxie, downloaded from www.twopeasinabucket.com.

quick idea: Turn your photo anchors into flower petals and arrange them in a fun flower design.

outlandish companion

Supplies *Patterned papers:* K&Company, Making Memories and Design Originals; *Foam stamps, eyelets and brads:* Making Memories; *Stamping ink:* Ranger Industries and Stampin' Up!; *Other:* Ribbon, metal pin and envelope.

quick idea: To complement my page theme, I wanted to use a piece of jewelry to represent a kilt pin. It was a little too dimensional for my liking, so I hammered it flat.

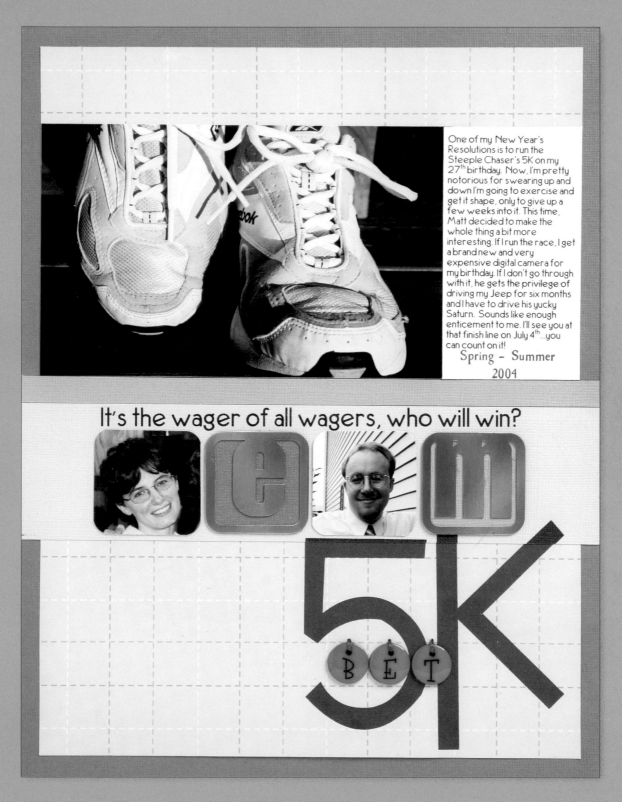

One of my New Year's Resolutions is to run the Steeple Chaser's 5K on my 27th birthday. Now, I'm pretty notorious for swearing up and down I'm going to exercise and get it shape, only to give up a few weeks into it. This time, Matt decided to make the whole thing a bit more interesting. If I run the race, I get a brand new and very expensive digital camera for my birthday. If I don't go through with it, he gets the privilege of driving my Jeep for six months and I have to drive his yucky Saturn. Sounds like enough enticement to me. I'll see you at that finish line on July 4th...you can count on it!

Spring – Summer 2004

It's the wager of all wagers, who will win?

5K BET

5k bet

Supplies *Patterned paper:* KI Memories; *Alphabet buttons:* Junkitz; *Metal letter clips:* Scrapworks; *Stamps:* Making Memories; *Stamping ink:* Stampin' Up!; *Computer fonts:* 2Peas Tubby and 2Peas Squish, downloaded from *www.twopeasinabucket.com.*

quick idea: An easy design tip? Crop your photos to the same size as your other elements (in this case, the metal letter clips) to create a consistent look on your page.

These little ditties are like a bad penny...still popping into my head at the oddest times.

Childhood RHYMES

Jingle Bells, Batman smells,
Robin laid an egg,
Batmobile lost a wheel,
And Joker got away
HEY!

Big Mac, Filet of Fish,
Quarter Pounder
French Fries, RC Cola,
Thick Shakes, Sundaes,
and Apple Pies

beep beep

pals

Criss cross applesauce,
Spiders crawling up your back,
Bird turd...dripping down...
GOTCHA!

Great big globs of greasy,
grimey gopher guts, mutilated
monkey feet, chopped up
baby parakeet feet!

childhood rhymes

Supplies *Patterned papers:* Kay by Marcella for Target and KI Memories; *Stickers:* Creative Imaginations; *Eyelets and eyelet letter charm:* Making Memories; *Conchos:* Scrapworks; *Computer fonts:* CK 8 Ball, "Creative Clips & Fonts for Everyday Celebrations" CD and CK Neat Print, "Creative Clips & Fonts for Special Occasions" CD, *Creating Keepsakes*; Avant Garde BT, Corel WordPerfect; Georgia, Microsoft Word.

quick idea: Another circle-rimmed title! Note also how I strung eyelets across the black cord along the bottom of my page. Think about stringing eyelets on ribbon as well.

painted metal accents

Have a metal accent that's almost quite right but seems to be missing something? Guess what? You can modify an accent with just a bit of paint. I like to take a paintbrush and paint just parts of my metal accents. Like the little red hearts on this layout. Look how the red hearts just kind of unify the whole layout. Use a small paintbrush so you can apply just a little bit of paint where you need it. And if you mess up? No worries. Just wash off the paint and try again.

sunday morning & pecan waffles

Supplies *Patterned papers:* Provo Craft, K&Company, Chatterbox and Daisy D's Paper Co.; *Rub-ons, acrylic paint and eyelets:* Making Memories; *Stickers:* SEI; *Computer font:* CK Chemistry, "Fresh Fonts" CD, *Creating Keepsakes.*

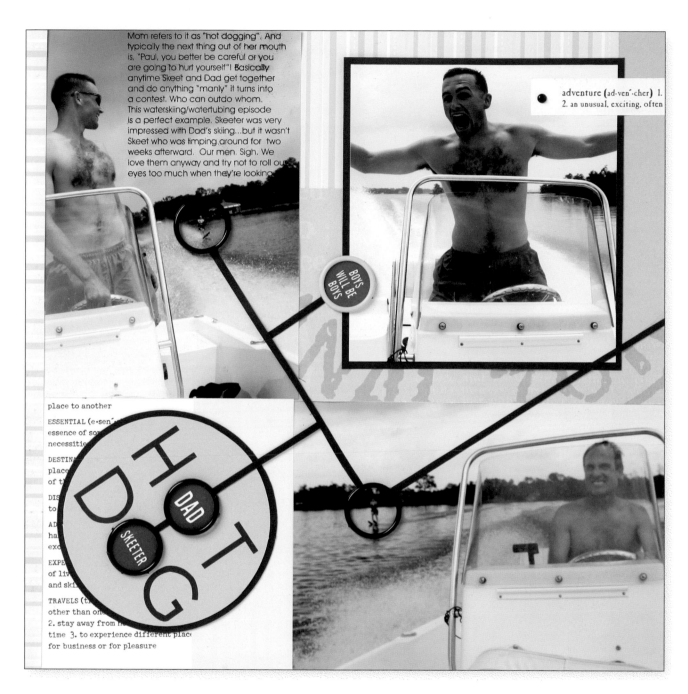

Mom refers to it as "hot dogging". And typically the next thing out of her mouth is, "Paul, you better be careful or you are going to hurt yourself"! Basically anytime Skeet and Dad get together and do anything "manly" it turns into a contest. Who can outdo whom. This waterskiing/watertubing episode is a perfect example. Skeeter was very impressed with Dad's skiing...but it wasn't Skeet who was limping around for two weeks afterward. Our men. Sigh. We love them anyway and try not to roll our eyes too much when they're looking.

adventure (ad·ven´·cher) 1.
2. an unusual, exciting, often

BOYS WILL BE BOYS

HOT DG

DAD

SKEETER

place to another

ESSENTIAL (e·sen´
essence of sor
necessities

DESTIN
place
of t

DIS
to

AD
ha
exc

EXPE
of liv
and ski

TRAVELS (t
other than on
2. stay away from h
time 3. to experience different place
for business or for pleasure

hot dog

Supplies *Patterned papers:* EK Success and K&Company; *Stickers and brads:* Making Memories; *Conchos:* Scrapworks; *Computer fonts:* 2Peas Tasklist and 2Peas Tubby, downloaded from *www.twopeasinabucket.com*; Avant Garde, Corel WordPerfect.

quick idea: Insert printed cardstock circles inside metal-rimmed tags to create visually interesting titles that will move your reader's eye across the page.

scrapbooker's night off

Supplies *Patterned papers:* Karen Foster Design, K&Company and Daisy D's Paper Co.; *Letter stamps:* Fusion Art Rubber Stamps; *Stamping ink:* Stampin' Up!; *Ribbon:* C.M. Offray & Son; *Clips and snap:* Making Memories; *Other:* Carnival tickets.

quick idea: Who can resist these swirly little clips? I sure can't. In fact, I have packages of them. Why not use them to add dimension to your page background?

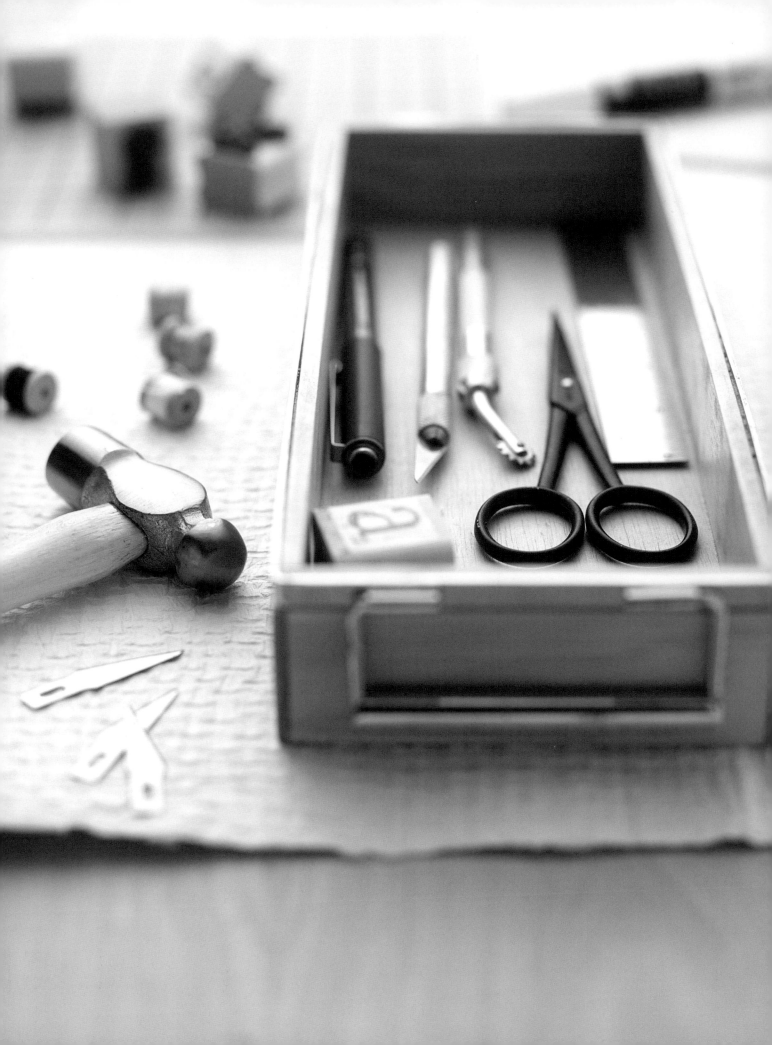

6.
tools

i heart

Supplies *Patterned papers:* Chatterbox and KI Memories; *Letter stamps:* Hero Arts; *Stamping ink:* Stampin' Up!; *Pens:* Zig Scroll & Brush, EK Success; Pigment Pro, American Crafts; *Punch:* EK Success; *Tacks:* Chatterbox; *Computer font:* Palatino Linotype, Microsoft Word.

chapter six

Have I mentioned yet that I love scrapbook supplies? I was so desperate for supplies at the start of my scrapbooking obsession that I took a part-time job at my local scrapbook store. I got paid in supplies. I thought it was great, and it definitely got my husband off my back about buying new products.

I accumulated all sorts of scrapbooking supplies and tools during this time period, including a fair share of punches. I don't care what anybody says, I'm in love with my punches. I still buy them. Bought a few new ones just a few weeks ago, come to think of it. They are classic, simple and just flat out tickle my fancy. And that punching-through-paper sound is just too satisfying. Don't you agree?

I was inspired to make this page when I walked by the front windows of an American Eagle Outfitters store. They had a hanging display of different patterned squares, each with a cutout of their eagle logo in the middle. Major light-bulb moment for me. I could use a punch instead of the logo. And now my logo is this little heart. Love it. No, no, no ... I heart it.

What kind of tools do you have in your scrapbooking stash? Pens? Circle cutters? Rubber stamps? Punches? More? In this chapter, I'll show you fun ideas for using the scrapbooking tools you already have.

remember the xyron?

I'm a new convert to interactive pages. Before, page protectors and I just didn't get along. What a nuisance they are, prohibiting my vision for my layout because they just hold everything away from hands. Logically, I see the appeal. They just don't jibe with my desire to have things to touch, to explore, to open up and see.

I've found a solution that solved all my problems: magnetic strips. I place magnetic strips on the back of my interactive elements and in the corresponding areas on my layout. The layout goes in the protector, and the magnets hold all the fun stuff in place on the outside. In this case, these little puzzle pieces are moveable. Rearrange them, solve the puzzle, see what they say. And all the other interactive pages in this book utilize the magnets in various other ways. Cool, huh? I have conquered the page protector.

Because I knew these puzzle pieces were going to be handled, I ran them through my Xyron. Remember that thing? That little, gray, funny-looking box in your scrap closet? It was a must-have at one time. Still have that laminating cartridge? I do. I used it to laminate those pieces. Now they're safe from direct handling as well as from little hands!

Where the? But what if I? **No, no.** If this goes here... **There is nothing more satisfying than a good** PRESTO! PUZZLE. If it takes less than 20 minutes, it was too easy. More than a day... I feel **dumb.** Somewhere in the middle & **I AM THE MAN!**

Especially if there is someone around to be really impressed. That's where my wife comes in. She smiles nicely and says, "Wow...you're good". Yea, honey, I know. Now if only I could figure her out...she's the biggest puzzle of them all.

matt ♥'s puzzles

what do i say?

puzzles

Supplies *Patterned papers:* Colorbök and American Crafts; *Rub-ons:* KI Memories; *Chipboard letters:* Li'l Davis Designs; *Computer fonts:* Times New Roman, Microsoft Word and unknown; *Other:* Magnetic strips.

quick idea: If the colors of your die cuts are too bright for your layout, mute them with a sheet of vellum.

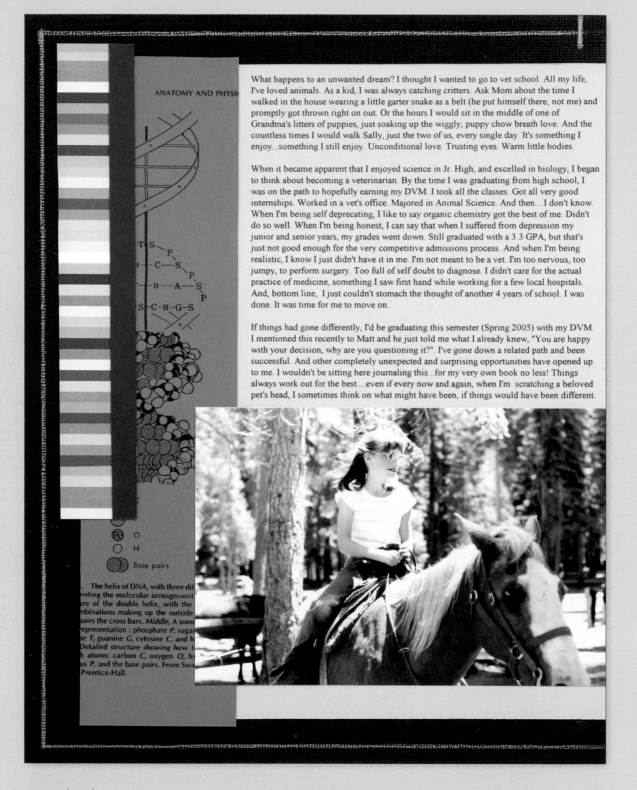

What happens to an unwanted dream? I thought I wanted to go to vet school. All my life, I've loved animals. As a kid, I was always catching critters. Ask Mom about the time I walked in the house wearing a little garter snake as a belt (he put himself there, not me) and promptly got thrown right on out. Or the hours I would sit in the middle of one of Grandma's litters of puppies, just soaking up the wiggly, puppy chow breath love. And the countless times I would walk Sally, just the two of us, every single day. It's something I enjoy...something I still enjoy. Unconditional love. Trusting eyes. Warm little bodies.

When it became apparent that I enjoyed science in Jr. High, and excelled in biology, I began to think about becoming a veterinarian. By the time I was graduating from high school, I was on the path to hopefully earning my DVM. I took all the classes. Got all very good internships. Worked in a vet's office. Majored in Animal Science. And then....I don't know. When I'm being self deprecating, I like to say organic chemistry got the best of me. Didn't do so well. When I'm being honest, I can say that when I suffered from depression my junior and senior years, my grades went down. Still graduated with a 3.3 GPA, but that's just not good enough for the very competitive admissions process. And when I'm being realistic, I know I just didn't have it in me. I'm not meant to be a vet. I'm too nervous, too jumpy, to perform surgery. Too full of self doubt to diagnose. I didn't care for the actual practice of medicine, something I saw first hand while working for a few local hospitals. And, bottom line, I just couldn't stomach the thought of another 4 years of school. I was done. It was time for me to move on.

If things had gone differently, I'd be graduating this semester (Spring 2005) with my DVM. I mentioned this recently to Matt and he just told me what I already knew, "You are happy with your decision, why are you questioning it?". I've gone down a related path and been successful. And other completely unexpected and surprising opportunities have opened up to me. I wouldn't be sitting here journaling this...for my very own book no less! Things always work out for the best....even if every now and again, when I'm scratching a beloved pet's head, I sometimes think on what might have been, if things would have been different.

vet school

Supplies *Patterned paper:* KI Memories; *Stickers:* Mustard Moon; *Letter stamps:* MoBe' Stamps and Fusion Art Rubber Stamps; *Colored pencils:* Crayola; *File folders:* Autumn Leaves; *Other:* Key ring.

quick idea: I traced a preprinted file folder to create unique page accents. Think about other cool uses for your disposable supplies.

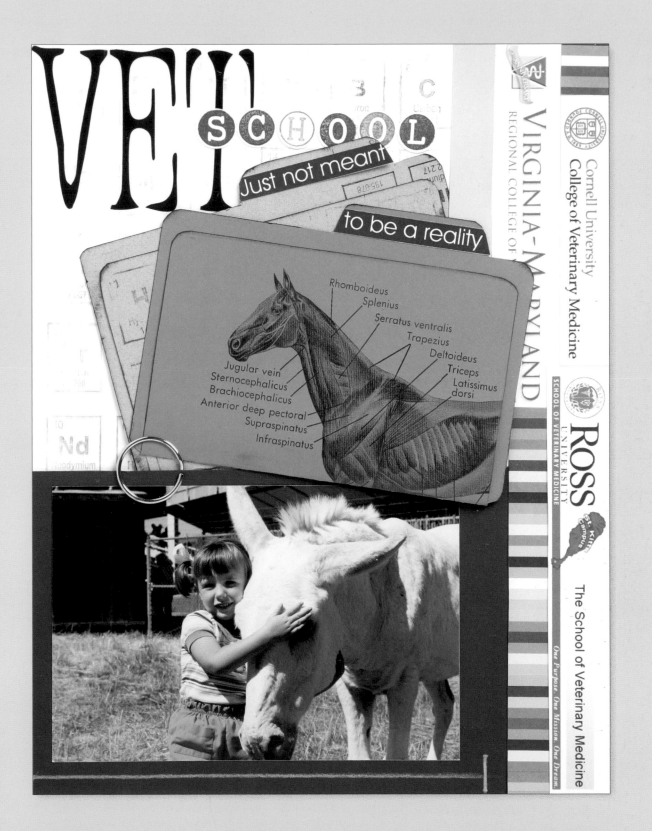

creative scraplifting

Shhhh! In addition to the other supplies I've just got to have, I also collect idea books. I believe that idea books are tools you can use for your pages, and you know what? I still refer back to my older idea books.

Pull out your old idea books and look at the layouts with a new focus. Don't look at the products or what you might think are outdated techniques, but rather observe the balance, the color, the journaling approaches.

Chances are you'll find something that appeals to you, as I did here with a Danelle Johnson layout from an older CK publication, *The Big Idea Book of Seasonal Memories*. Instead of scraplifting it exactly, I let it inspire me. I turned it 90 degrees, used the latest and greatest paper I could get my hands on, and just let my imagination take me where it wanted.

touch the autumn
by Danelle Johnson, as featured in *The Big Idea Book of Seasonal Memories* by Creating Keepsakes

Supplies *Patterned papers:* Scrappin' Dreams; *Fibers:* Fibers & Yarns & Threads, Oh My!, Rubba Dub Dub; *Pop dots:* All Night Media; *Computer fonts:* Rubberstamp, Artlookin and BN Font Boy, downloaded from the Internet.

because Skeeter flew more than kites in Pensacola

2004

sea sand life Fly

Kites rise highest against the wind...not with it. –Sir Winston Churchill

sea, sand, life, fly

Supplies *Patterned papers:* BasicGrey; *Tags and brad:* Making Memories; *Rub-ons:* Chartpak and Making Memories; *Stickers:* Creative Imaginations; *Computer font:* CK Fraternity, "Creative Clips & Fonts by Becky Higgins" CD, *Creating Keepsakes.*

When watching hockey and they score a goal say .....

In golf, a "hole in one" is a....

When watching baseball and a player hits it out of the park, say

STRIKE!

slam dunk

play

Instead of saying "foul ball" in baseball, say...

fore!

touch down

Truth be told, I can be one annoying wife. I've learned that sometimes, it is more fun to start pushing buttons than it is to play nice. One of my favorite things to do is mix up all my sports references when Matt's watching his favorite sports. For a really smart girl, I sure can play dumb! What can I say, I'm talented!

A soccer pass is referred to as a....

inside

SLAP SHOT

SPOIL SPORT

A basket in basketball is called a .....

SPORTS

S

game

goal

10/00

spoil sport

Supplies *Patterned papers, vellum and stickers:* American Crafts; *Snaps:* Making Memories; *Computer font:* 2Peas Tubby, downloaded from *www.twopeasinabucket.com*.

quick idea: My computer is a great tool that I love to use for creating pages. For this page, I used a word-processing program to create the grids and the journaling.

tricks with zig markers

Would you be surprised if I told you that I had the entire sets of
Zig Writers and Zig Scroll & Brush Markers? Oh, don't ask me
why—I'm not really into creative lettering. I think maybe I like the look
of the markers all neatly lined up in rainbow order in their cases. I've used
them on occasion but never really enough to justify the cost … until now.

This layout is a great example of how to take a tool, like a marker, and use it in a
creative way. I used a marker in conjunction with a circle punch, a ruler and the inside of
a tape roll (conveniently sitting on my desk) to create a clean and subtle look on my page.
And I'm in love with how easy it was. Give it a try.

28

Supplies *Textured cardstock:*
DieCuts with a View; *Patterned
papers:* Cross-My-Heart and Karen
Foster Design; *Stickers:* Colorbök;
Rub-ons: KI Memories; *Brad:*
Junkitz; *Punch:* McGill; *Pen:* Zig
Writer, EK Success; *Computer font:*
AL Uncle Charles, "Essential Fonts"
CD, Autumn Leaves.

One summer night, when the one that I wanted was home, hopelessly devoted to a game of poker, I hung out with these two lovebirds at the city park. "Grease" was playing for Frederick City's 1st Summer Nite Cinema. I've said it before and I'll say it again....I love Frederick. Love all the things there are to do, especially in the summer. The local radio station was involved and there was a 50's costume contest (in fact, we were all encouraged to show up in costume), a soda fountain was set up in the band shell, and classic cars where on display. At dusk, we were treated to a free movie. Even though it was late June, it got pretty darn cold and Danny was such a gentleman by trying to give us his coat! We still froze. Which made me all the more prepared when we went back in September to see E.T...that time with sleeping bags& Reese's Pieces.

summer nite cinema

Supplies *Patterned papers:* SEI and Karen Foster Design; *Letter stamps:* Stamp Cabana; *Stamping ink:* Stampin' Up!; *Stickers:* SEI; *Punch:* All Night Media; *Other:* Liner notes.

quick idea: I made my own "photo negative strip" with my filmstrip punch and a piece of black cardstock.

I am a lover of summer. My entire calendar revolves around it. October through April are just wasted months, a means to getting back to warm, playful days. So, when the leaves turn, inside I'm screaming at them to stop...stay green just a little longer... no need to go away! I resign myself to the shortened days, sad inside there is less sunlight to enjoy after dinner. Pumpkins and foliage do nothing to console me. Mere bandaids on my wounded

thoughts. I've wondered if I would happy living in a climate with a perpetual summer. Florida? Southern California? Probably not. It's the absence of something that makes it more loved. And so, I continue to weather the winter. Long dreary and cold days that will eventually bring be make to the thing I love the most.

fall

Supplies *Patterned papers:* Scenic Route Paper Co. and Provo Craft; *Transparency:* Karen Foster Design; *Letter stamps:* Ma Vinci's Reliquary; *Stamping ink:* ColorBox, Clearsnap; *Colored pencils:* Crayola; *Charm:* Once Upon a Charm; *Metal accent:* EK Success; *Circle cutter:* Coluzzle, Provo Craft; *Computer font:* AL Uncle Charles, "Essential Fonts" CD, Autumn Leaves.

quick idea: You never know when a circle cutter (or a circle template) might come in handy. Circles are versatile design elements that help move your eye across the page.

Tiger
&
Fuss-Fuss

MOM & THEN

One of each. Just the two of them. Brother and Sister. Now, Chrissy is expecting her second. The interval between Baby Brown and little Ruthie will be almost the same as between these two. A fact that is not lost on anybody. History repeats itself...Lincoln style.

tiger & fuss-fuss

Supplies *Patterned papers:* American Crafts; *Embossing template:* Stampin' Up!; *Letter stamps:* FontWerks; *Stamping ink:* Ranger Industries; *Punches:* McGill and EK Success; *Micro-eyelets and safety pins:* Making Memories; *Computer font:* AL Uncle Charles, "Essential Fonts" CD, Autumn Leaves; *Other:* Ribbon.

step-by-step:
plastic template tricks

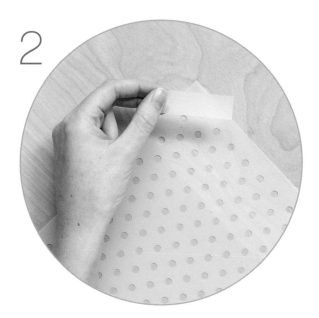

It sometimes amazes me when I look at everything I bought before I even knew what I really liked.

I'm sure I had a project in mind when I bought this plastic embossing template from Stampin' Up!. I was glad to find it in my closet, though. Polka-dot patterns are so hot right now. And do I have to use it to emboss? Nope! I was really excited when I realized I could take a hole punch and use the template to position the punches on my page.

Here's how to do it:

1. Place a piece of cardstock on your work surface and position the plastic embossing template over the cardstock.

2. Use temporary adhesive (I steal the painter's tape out of my hubby's workshop) to adhere your template to your work surface. The impact of the punch might cause the template to "jump," and you'll be constantly repositioning to keep the design straight. Just avoid the frustration and tape it down before you start the project.

3. Use the template to guide the position of your hole punches.

let sleeping dogs lie

Supplies *Patterned papers:* K&Company; *Rub-ons, bookplate, metal letters and foam stamps:* Making Memories; *Stamping ink:* Stampin' Up!; *Chalk:* Craf-T Products; *Stickers:* Creative Imaginations; *Computer font:* AL Uncle Charles, "Essential Fonts" CD, Autumn Leaves.

quick idea. I stamped the word "Secrets" all over the circle until the actual word is lost within the background.

parenthood

Supplies *Patterned papers:* Scrapworks; *Stickers:* American Crafts; *Letter stamps:* Hero Arts; *Stamp positioner:* Stamp-a-ma-jig, EK Success; *Stamping ink:* Ranger Industries and Stampin' Up!; *Brads:* Junkitz; *Pen:* Pigment Pro, American Crafts; *Computer font:* 2Peas Tubby, downloaded from *www.twopeasinabucket.com*; *Other:* Circle rubber stamp.

quick idea. I used a ruler and stamp positioner to line up the design of my circle rubber stamps on this page. You could also paint through a polka-dot template for a similar look.

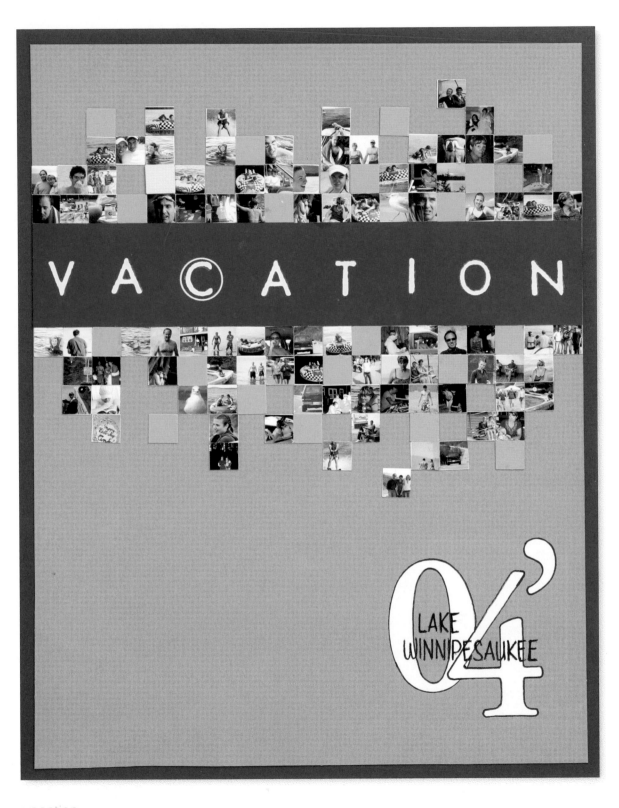

vacation

Supplies *Stickers:* American Crafts; *Rub-ons:* KI Memories and Making Memories; *Punch:* EK Success; *Pen:* Pigment Pro, American Crafts; *Computer font:* AL Meaningful, "Script Fonts" CD, Autumn Leaves.
quick idea: I used my tiny little square punch on my index prints to create the look on this page. Of course, now I'm wondering what a tiny circle punch could do.

Baby, every little piece of the puzzle doesn't always fit

PERFECTLY

Love can be rough around the edges, tattered at the seams
But Honey, if it's good enough for you, it's good enough for me
If your mother doesn't like the way I treat her baby boy
If in every wedding picture, my daddy looks annoyed
It's alright, it's alright
Don't you know that all the fairy tales tell a lie
Real love and real life doesn't have to be perfect
You don't mind if I show up late for everything
And when you lose your cool, it's kinda cute to me
Ain't it nice to know that we don't have to be perfect?

ON A LOVER'S GETAWAY IT'S ALRIGHT IF I RATHER WEAR YOUR T SHIRT THAN A SEXY NEGLIGEE IT'S ALRIGHT IF YOU DON'T TAKE ME TO PARIS

Erin and Matt Erin and Matt Erin and

NEGLIGEE IT'S ALRIGHT EVERY DINNER DOESN'T

Verse 2 & 3 **[Perfect]** Verse 1
by Sara Evans

HAVE TO BE CANDLELIGHT IT DOESN'T HAVE TO BE PERFECT, IT'S KINDA NICE TO KNOW THAT IT

This is our song. When it comes on the radio. I sing it at the top of my lungs with a smile on my face. because I know it's message rings true for us Perfectly OK with being imperfect.

perfect

Supplies *Patterned papers:* Two Busy Moms and Patchwork Paper Design; *Journaling template:* Chatterbox for EK Success; *Letter stamps:* PSX Design; *Stamping ink:* Stampin' Up!; *Punches:* EK Success; *Buttons:* Making Memories; *Computer fonts:* AL Featherbrained, "Handwritten Fonts" CD, Autumn Leaves; Times New Roman, Microsoft Word; 2Peas Think Small, downloaded from *www.twopeasinabucket.com; Other:* Ribbon.

step-by-step: new life
for journaling templates

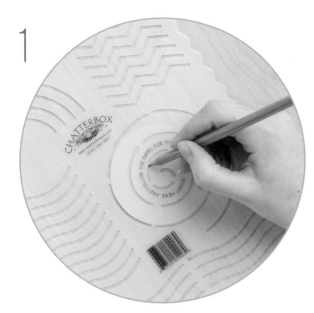

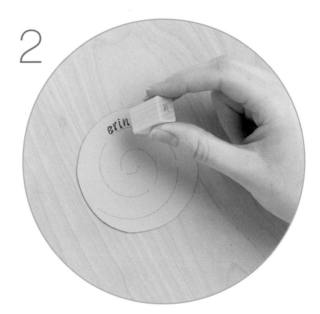

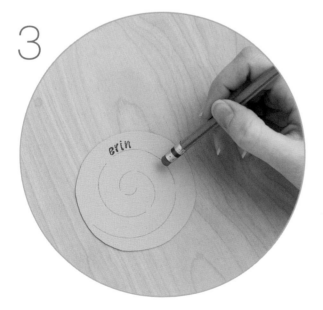

I think I would rather pull out my teeth than hand-journal. That's not to say I don't see its value. It's just that I'm so inept at it. Two left hands. I decided long ago that I wasn't going to give myself a headache over it when I had a computer, a printer and a smorgasbord of free fonts online.

Life's too short for that, my friends. And so I was left with journaling templates and no desire ever to use them again. Until I suddenly realized I could use them to position my small rubber stamps on my page. Oh, boy. Take a look at this.

Here's how to do it:
1. Trace your journaling-template shape on your layout with a pencil.
2. Using your pencil marks as a guide, position your stamps to create your journaling.
3. Erase the pencil lines.

note: *Flip and rotate your journaling template for added interest in your design.*

hold on tight

Supplies *Patterned paper, acrylic paint and snaps:* Making Memories; *Computer fonts:* Compata BD Bt, Corel WordPerfect; CK Evolution, "Fresh Fonts" CD, *Creating Keepsakes; Other:* Foam stamp.

quick idea: Use a word-processing program to convert a font into an outline font. After printing it out, use paint as a fill for a more dramatic effect.

play

Supplies *Patterned papers:* KI Memories and Marcella by Kay for Target; *Letter and word die cuts and concho:* Scrapworks; *Buttons and snaps:* Making Memories; *Acrylic accent:* KI Memories; *Decorative scissors:* Provo Craft; *Computer fonts:* 2Peas Chemistry, "Fresh Fonts" CD, *Creating Keepsakes; Other:* Ribbon.

quick idea: Create a quick and easy frame using your computer. I used Microsoft Excel to create this frame, printed it out and simply trimmed with a decorative scissors.

tool revival 101

One of my very first tool purchases was Puzzle Mates' Magic Matter. It includes four little metal disks of varying diameters. When rolled along the edge of a photo with a pencil in the center hole, it creates the perfect size mat for your photograph. You just grab a pencil and trim away.

I've long ago retired that look and have since found easier ways to mat my photos. I never did get rid of it though—and guess what? It proved to be the perfect solution on this page. I wanted to outline my photographs to help them pop against the color-blocked background. So, I loaded the Magic Matter with a colored pencil and outlined my photographs.

You may not have a Magic Matter in your supply collection, but take a moment and think about the creative possibilities with other old tools you just had to have. (Believe me, I can think of a few that I thought I couldn't live without.)

bug eating 101

Supplies *Patterned paper:* American Crafts; *Letter stamps:* Ma Vinci's Reliquary; *Stamping ink:* Stampin' Up!; *Bingo numbers:* Li'l Davis Designs; *Colored pencils:* Crayola; *Matting tool:* Magic Matter, Puzzle Mates; *Computer fonts:* Times New Roman, Microsoft Word; AL Uncle Charles, "Essential Fonts" CD, Autumn Leaves.

1993 to 2003

10 years in maryland

Supplies *Patterned paper and stickers:* Chatterbox; *Snaps:* Making Memories; *Computer font:* Times New Roman, Microsoft Word.
quick idea: I needed a Maryland state flag for this page. I found one online, downloaded it, enlarged it and printed it out.

A lot of things were going through our minds that cold December morning as we flew across country, each of us kids in our own window seat, but I'm sure the prospect of a long term future in Maryland was not one of them. Our previous nomadic existence didn't allow for us to linger in one town for too long and we all thought that Maryland was just another stepping stone in the journey. Ten years later, we are all a bit surprised to still be here. Along the way we've all graduated high school, have three degrees from state colleges under our belts, and a new family member in Matthew. Mom and Dad remain in the house they built themselves and Dad has achieved a few career goals. We can get around the majority of the state without having to glance at a map and a few of us can even eat crabs like natives. Granted, the old west wind does blow our way occasionally, making us long for the mountains and open spaces of our past, but for now we are staying to extend our unprecedented residency of what we now consider to be home.

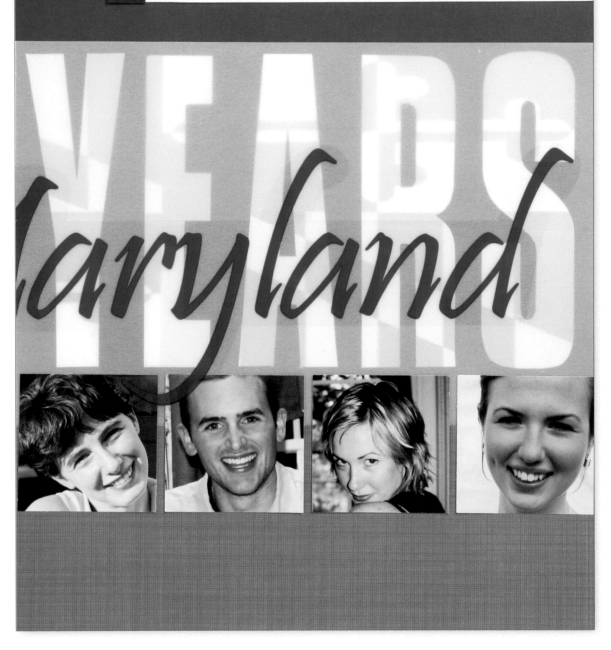

forgotten templates

I am in love with this lettering template. Where has it been all this time? Lost. Neglected. Forgotten about in a binder full of supplies I thought I didn't want. Thank goodness, I rescued it. It's going back in my "favorite supplies" pile. To freshen up the look, I mainly used it just to outline my letters on cardstock in a funky background design and then filled the letters in with a little bit of light-gray shading. Then I added a little punch with a title cut out of bright-colored cardstock.

goofy

Supplies *Lettering template:* Pebbles for EK Success; *Rub-ons:* Doodlebug Design; *Punch:* All Night Media; *Pens:* Pigment Pro, American Crafts; Zig Scroll & Brush, EK Success; *Eyelets and charms:* Making Memories.

lazy & relaxed

Supplies *Patterned paper and stickers:* Pebbles Inc.; *Letter stamps:* Fusion Art Rubber Stamps, Ma Vinci's Reliquary, PSX Design and Rubber Moon Stamp Company; *Stamping ink:* Stampin' Up! and Clearsnap.

quick idea Gotta love my extensive collection of rubber stamps. I put them all to good use to hand-stamp this page background.

fun factoids

fun factoids

Supplies *Patterned paper, stickers and buttons:* American Crafts; *Punch:* EK Success; *Computer font:* 2Peas Tasklist, downloaded from *www.twopeasinabucket.com.*
quick idea: I printed my journaling on cardstock first, then punched it into tag shapes and added the tags to my layout.